Nature's Harvest

the vegetable cookbook

Arabella Boxer

Henry Regnery Company, Chicago

Library of Congress Cataloging in Publication Data
Boxer, Lady Arabella.
    Nature's harvest: the vegetable cookbook.

    1. Cookery (Vegetables)   I. Title.
TX801.B69   641.6'5   73-20672
ISBN 0-8092-8911-3
ISBN 0-8092-8380-8 (pbk.)

Published by Henry Regnery Company
114 West Illinois Street, Chicago, Illinois 60610
Manufactured in the United States of America
Library of Congress Catalog Card Number: 73-20672
International Standard Book Number: 0-8092-8911-3 (cloth)
                                    0-8092-8380-8 (paper)

Contents

Preface

My preference for vegetables has grown steadily over the past four or five years for several reasons, and I cannot help thinking there must be many others who feel as I do. I believe the main reason I prefer vegetables is that they make such beautiful material with which to work, whether gathered from one's own garden or selected with care at the grocery. There is also the pleasure of choosing vegetables, seeing each week what has newly come into season, and rejecting what has passed its peak. Unlike the butcher's shop, where the produce varies little from season to season, the greengrocer is a constant reminder of the passing months, and as each new root, leaf and fruit makes its appearance, so a dish that is relevant to that particular moment suggests itself.

The rising costs of beef and fish have added to my interest in vegetables. Instead of experimenting with cheaper cuts, I find that I have done the opposite and now think of meat and fish as a luxury. More and more frequently, I use vegetables as main courses, and I only occasionally treat myself to good cuts of meats and fish. I buy poultry more often, partly because chicken combines so well with vegetable dishes and partly because I rely on a regular supply of chicken stock.

The rest of the time I live on dishes made from combinations of vegetables with pastry, rice, noodles, cheese or eggs, gnocchi or pancakes. I do not claim to save much time or money by eating in this way, for accumulating a varied selection of vegetables is not always cheap, and there is some work involved, although I find the preparation is pleasant.

Perhaps this book will alter the reader's thinking about the role of vegetables in a meal. The American and English habit of serving vegetables only as side dishes has resulted in their rather unimaginative treatment. The French custom of serving vegetables as a separate course, usually following the meat course, has resulted in a greater respect for vegetables in that country. But it is probably in the Chinese cuisine that vegetables are most profitably and attractively served. In a Chinese meal, each food is treated with equal importance. A dish of bamboo sprouts that have been grown in the kitchen are given the same care as a lobster dish. A dish of meat or fish is included among a selection of other foods, or a small quantity of meat or fish is cooked with equal amounts of vegetables.

As you explore vegetable cooking, you may want to serve an all-vegetable meal. Vegetables complement each other and benefit from being served in combinations of two or three. At the end of the book there are suggested menus planned around all-vegetable meals.

I am by no means a strict vegetarian. Many of the dishes in this book contain a small amount of meat, but it is the proportion that is different: meat is used as an accessory rather than a focal point of the meal. A stuffed cabbage may contain some minced meat, a dish of green beans may be garnished with chopped bacon, while a *risi e bisi* is much improved by a handful of chopped prosciutto. A ham bone gives more flavor and nourishment to a soup of dried peas, while duck fat or beef dripping adds an excellent flavor and improved texture to a dish of dried lentils or haricot beans. I like to make most soups with chicken or veal stock, although vegetable stock can be used and vegetable stock cubes are even available in health food stores.

I hope this book will encourage more people to experiment in the realm of vegetable cookery, and to extend their range of vegetable dishes.

Arabella Boxer
England

[1]

Getting Ready to Cook

Perhaps because of the fragility of the vegetable flavors, the choice of other ingredients seems to be vital. Recipes indicate the combination of other foods with vegetables. Also of importance are the fats and oils in which vegetable dishes are cooked, as well as the herbs and flavorings used to season them.

Fats and oils. Margarine is adequate for the actual cooking of vegetables and is often used for reasons of diet or economy, but nothing can replace the taste of uncooked butter, preferably unsalted, melting over a dish of plainly boiled or steamed vegetables. Animal fats are excellent for certain purposes. Beef dripping works well for dishes of root vegetables or for dried vegetables, goose fat is invaluable for hearty vegetable soups, and chicken and duck fat are especially good for frying potatoes.

There are a variety of oils suitable for cooking with vegetables, although the two best are olive oil and sunflower-seed oil. Olive oil is good in salads and for cooking, where it should be mixed half and half with butter to keep the butter from burning. Sunflower-seed oil is also good for salads and for sautéing; it gives a lighter taste than olive oil and seems to suit certain foods better. Arachide (or nut) oil is a good substitute for sunflower-seed oil as it is also light and almost tasteless. For deep frying a mixture of arachide oil and sunflower-seed oil can be used.

Other oils that are good to have on hand include sesame, useful in preparing Middle Eastern dishes; almond and walnut, both excellent with salad greens such as chicory, endive and watercress. The walnut oil is the heaviest, and it is best mixed with a lighter oil for use in salad dressings.

White wine vinegar is excellent for cutting all the oils, and tarragon vinegar as a change. Red wine vinegar is mainly used in meat dishes.

Dairy products. Apart from butter there are several other dairy products which are invaluable in vegetable cookery. The whole range of creams, sour creams, yoghurts and buttermilk are extremely useful, especially for cold soups, uncooked sauces and dressings. When eating a lot of salads one needs to vary the dressings; anyone familiar with the hors-d'oeuvre tray in a moderate restaurant will know the monotony of a number of dishes dressed with the identical *vinaigrette*. With both raw salads and *salad composées* (those made with cooked vegetables), it is easy to make numerous variations with mixtures of yoghurt, sour cream, olive oil, cream and buttermilk.

Yoghurt is very good in uncooked dishes; in cooking it must be first treated to prevent it from separating and spoiling the appearance of the dish. The easiest way to do this is to mix a carton of yoghurt to a smooth paste with a teaspoonful of flour before adding it to a hot dish. In most of the recipes in this book, yoghurt, cream and sour cream are interchangeable, depending on your taste and the required degree of richness. Buttermilk is good in cold soups. A reasonable substitute for buttermilk can be made by mixing milk with sour cream and a little lemon juice.

All these products go well with vegetables; they seem to add a degree of richness and creaminess without the weight produced by quantities of cream. They are also healthier and much less fattening than pure cream, and have a pleasant tartness. They give to cold dishes what butter gives to hot dishes, a certain smoothness of texture, and they seem to bring out the individual flavor of the vegetable.

Seasoning. As for seasonings, sea salt and freshly ground black peppercorns are most important. Celery salt is an excellent flavoring, and there are several useful mixtures of pepper. Spices are of little use in preparing vegetables, with the exception of mace and nutmeg, both of which are excellent in cheese sauces, white sauces and some soups.

Citrus fruits such as lemons, oranges and limes provide juice to use in place of vinegar in salad dressings.

Utensils. A few utensils are essential to the preparation and the cooking of vegetables. A large wooden chopping surface, preferably teak, plus an extra chopping board, and two really good French steel knives, one very small, and one long one are basic for preparation. For the cooking, the following utensils are useful: two or three large steel saucepans with heavy bases; one very deep pot for making vegetable stocks; one large round cast iron casserole—for cooking dishes like sauerkraut in large quantities; one lidded sauté pan, invaluable for braising and stewing vegetables, and a skillet for frying. A steamer is very useful, especially for potatoes and fragile vegetables such as broccoli and cauliflower, but it can be improvised by using a colander or strainer inside a saucepan. A few luxuries, well worth buying but not essential, include a tall narrow pan for sauces; a small china bowl to fit in the top of the saucepan, for making delicate egg-based sauces like *hollandaise;* and one or two small saucepans with lids, for cooking or serving sauces or small amounts of vegetables.

The vegetable mill or *mouli-legumes* is a vital piece of equipment. The largest size is by far the most useful.

Every kitchen should possess a sieve and a pair of strainers, one round with a coarse mesh, and one conical with a very fine mesh. An electric blender is extremely useful for puréeing vegetables and for making smooth soups.

A juice extractor is probably a luxury considering the price in relation to the amount of use it usually gets. But it is a lovely thing to have; nothing is better than fresh tomato, apple or carrot juice when these foods are at their cheapest and most plentiful. It is also useful for feeding invalids and sick children as even small amounts of pure vegetable juice are extremely nourishing and appetizing.

As for serving vegetables, few things set them off better than pure white china. Vegetables are so colorful and make such attractive combinations, that decoration on the china often detracts from the appearance of the dish. Among colored chinas, however, oven-proof earthenware dishes, rectangular or oval, are ideal for all foods covered with sauces, and can be browned under the grill or in a quick oven without worry.

[2]

Soups

BEAN SOUP

½ pound dried haricot beans
2 carrots
2 leeks
2 stalks celery
½ pound tomatoes
4 tablespoons olive oil
4 cups bean stock
salt and black pepper
chopped parsley

Soak the dried beans for 2 hours, then cook gently in simmering water until they are tender (1—2 hours, depending on their age). Add salt only towards the end of cooking. Reserve four cups of the liquid for stock. Chop the carrots, leeks, celery and peeled tomatoes. Heat the oil in a heavy pan and brown the leeks in it, adding the carrots, celery and tomatoes at intervals of about 3 minutes. When all are slightly softened and golden, pour in the reheated stock. Bring to boiling point and cook until the vegetables are tender (about 20 minutes). Stir in the beans and reheat. Season to taste

with plenty of salt and coarsely ground black pepper. Sprinkle with chopped parsley, or have a bowl of it on the table.
    Serves 6.

This makes a very substantial soup for cold weather; for a less thick soup use ¼ pound of beans.

ICED BEET SOUP

2 raw beets
1 cucumber
2½ cups beef or duck stock
2 tablespoons lemon juice
2 tablespoons white wine vinegar
1 cup thin cream

Peel the beets and chop into small pieces. Cook in 5 cups of lightly salted water until tender—about 1½ hours. Peel and slice the cucumber. Add it to the beets and cook for another 5 minutes. Put the mixture through the fine mesh of a vegetable mill or purée in the blender, gradually adding a pint of beef stock. Season with 2—4 tablespoons lemon juice, or 2 tablespoons lemon juice and 2 tablespoons white wine vinegar. Chill for several hours or overnight. Pour into a chilled tureen and swirl in the cream—don't mix it in too thoroughly, as it looks prettier with a marbled effect. This makes 4 pints.
    Serves 10—12.

BORSCHT

3 tablespoons butter
1 large onion
2 large beets
2—3 carrots, depending on size
2 stalks celery
2 cloves garlic (optional)
4 large tomatoes
1 bunch parsley
8 cups beef or chicken and beef stock mixed
salt and black pepper
2 cloves
1 bay leaf
1—2 tablespoons lemon juice
½ cup sour cream

Chop the onion, cut the beets and carrots *en julienne,* slice the celery, mince the garlic, skin and chop the tomatoes. Melt the butter in a large deep soup pot and cook the onion until it starts to soften and color. Add the beets, carrots and celery. Cook gently for 10 minutes, stirring now and then. Add the tomatoes and garlic and cook another 5 minutes, then pour in the heated stock. Bring to a boil, lower the heat, and add salt and black pepper, parsley, cloves and bay leaf. Simmer gently for 1½ hours. Remove the herbs, add more salt and black pepper, a pinch of sugar, and lemon juice to taste. Serve in a tureen or in individual bowls. Serve sour cream separately.

Serves 6–8

For a cold borscht, strain and chill overnight in the refrigerator. Serve with sour cream.

CELERIAC AND CARROT SOUP

1 pound celeriac
½ pound carrots
5 cups chicken stock
3 tablespoons butter
¼ cup cream
chopped parsley

Peel the celeriac, cut in pieces and cover with half the chicken stock. Scrape and slice the carrots into chunks and cover with the remaining chicken stock. Cook about 20 minutes or until tender. Drain the vegetables and reserve the stock or water. Push the celeriac, carrot and a small amount of the stock through a vegetable mill or purée in a blender and return to a clean pan. Add the chicken stock to the puréed vegetables and reheat. Season to taste with salt and black pepper, and stir in the cream and butter. Serve in bowls sprinkled with chopped parsley.

Serves 6.

CELERIAC SOUP

1 pound celeriac
½ pound potatoes
4 tablespoons butter or beef drippings
4 cups beef or chicken stock

salt and black pepper
¼ cup cream
chopped parsley

Peel the celeriac and cut in cubes. Peel the potatoes and cut in thin slices. Melt the butter in a heavy saucepan and cook the celeriac in it for 5 minutes. Add the sliced potatoes, stir until well mixed, and add the heated stock. Bring to a boil, cover the pan and simmer until both vegetables are soft, about 30 minutes. Put through the medium mesh of the vegetable mill and return to a clean pan. Reheat, stir in the cream and add salt and black pepper to taste. Serve with a bowl of chopped parsley on the table, or sprinkle a little in each bowl.

Serves 4–6.

CHERVIL SOUP

4 cups hot chicken stock
1½ tablespoons butter
1 tablespoon flour
1 bunch chervil (2–3 sprigs)
1 egg yolk
1 tablespoon lemon juice
salt and black pepper

Melt the butter, stir in the flour and pour in the heated stock. Stir until blended and simmer gently for about 3 minutes. Add the chervil and set aside for about 30 minutes. Beat the egg yolk and lemon juice in a small bowl. Remove the chervil from the stock and reheat to the boiling point. Mix a couple of tablespoonfuls of the boiling stock with the egg and lemon mixture, then add to the rest of the stock. Stir over low heat for a few minutes. Do not boil.

Serves 4.

This soup can also be made with tarragon.

CORN CHOWDER

6 ears corn-on-the-cob
1 large onion
1 leek
2 ounces salt pork or bacon fat

3½ cups milk
2½ cups chicken stock
½ cup thin cream
chopped parsley
soda crackers or matzos (optional)
black pepper

Cut the corn off the cobs with a small sharp knife, holding the cobs down-ward on a chopping board. Chop the onion and slice the leek. Dice the salt pork and fry gently until crisp in a heavy casserole. When it has rendered enough fat, add the chopped onion and stir for 1–2 minutes. Add the leek and continue to cook gently for another 2–3 minutes. Add the corn and stir until well coated with fat. Heat the stock and the milk together and pour into the casserole. Bring just to boiling point, taste for seasoning—it will prob-ably only need pepper because of the salt pork—and let soup simmer for 20 minutes. Add the cream, sprinkle with chopped parsley, and serve with soda crackers or matzos.
    Serves 8–10.

This soup can be made even more substantial by adding 2 diced potatoes at the same time as the corn.

FENNEL SOUP

1 head fennel
4 cups chicken stock
1 tablespoon white wine vinegar
salt and white pepper
1 ounce coarsely ground almonds (optional)

Wash and trim the fennel, reserving any of the feathery leaves. Slice it and put in a pan with the stock and the vinegar. Bring to the boil and simmer un-til the fennel is soft. For a delicious clear consommé simmer for 30 minutes, then strain the soup and reheat it, tasting for seasoning. Sharpen with a drop of extra vinegar if it seems too bland. Chop the reserved leaves and use as a garnish. For a slightly thicker soup, simmer for 20 minutes, then cool slightly. Put in the blender, return to the cleaned pan and reheat, adding salt and pepper to taste. Sprinkle with almonds to add texture. Top with finely chopped leaves.
    Serves 4–6.

This soup freezes well, without the garnish.

GARLIC SOUP

5 cloves garlic
4 tablespoons butter
1½ tablespoons flour
4 cups chicken stock
salt
6 black peppercorns
½ bay leaf
¼ teaspoon mace
3 cloves
1 egg yolk
1 tablespoon olive oil
3 tablespoons finely chopped parsley

Mince the garlic and cook gently in the butter until soft, about 4 minutes. Be careful not to burn it. Stir in the flour, and cook for another 3 minutes, stirring constantly. Heat the stock and add to the garlic mixture. Bring to a boil, then lower the heat. Add salt, peppercorns, cloves, bay leaf and mace. Simmer for 25 minutes. Pour through a strainer. Beat the egg yolk in a hot tureen. Stir in the oil drop by drop. When blended, pour in the hot soup. Stir till smooth, add the chopped parsley and serve.

Serves 3—4.

An unusual soup with a subtle flavor that is not liked by everyone, but well worth trying.

GAZPACHO

1 pound tomatoes
1 medium onion
1 green pepper
½ cucumber
2 cloves garlic
2 slices brown bread
½ cup tomato juice
1 cup chicken stock or water
¼ cup olive oil
2 tablespoons wine vinegar
salt and black pepper
ice cubes

Skin the tomatoes and chop finely, discarding seeds and juice. Chop the onion finely. Remove the pith and seeds from the pepper and chop. Peel the cucumber and cut in small dice. Mince the garlic. Remove the crusts from the bread, and dice. Put everything in a large bowl and add the tomato juice, stock or water, oil and vinegar. Mix and season with salt and black pepper. Chill for several hours, or overnight. Thin with ice cubes and iced water to the desired consistency before serving.
    Serves 8.

For a smooth version, the soup can be put in the blender. If made in the blender, have small bowls of very finely chopped cucumber, tomato, green pepper and hard-boiled egg as garnishes.

COLD LENTIL SOUP

¾ cup brown lentils
¼ pound spinach
1 onion
1 clove garlic
2 tablespoons sunflower-seed oil
salt and black pepper
2 cups buttermilk, approximately
½ lemon

Wash the lentils carefully and cover with cold water. Bring to a boil and cook gently until almost tender, about 45 minutes. Wash and slice the spinach. Add the spinach to the lentils and cook for another 15 minutes, or until both vegetables are tender. Chop the onion and garlic and sauté in the oil, adding the garlic about 5 minutes after the onion. When golden, add onion, garlic and the oil to the rest of the soup. Purée in the blender, pour into a bowl and chill. When cold, stir in the buttermilk. There should be 2–3 parts soup to 1 of buttermilk. Add lemon juice to taste. Serve very cold.
    Serves 6–8.

This is a delicious and unusual summer soup; the combination of flavors is excellent, and it makes a quite substantial start to a light meal.

LETTUCE AND HAZELNUT SOUP

3 heads of lettuce
1 bunch scallions or one medium onion
4 tablespoons butter

3 cups light stock—chicken, veal or vegetable
4 tablespoons thin cream
4 tablespoons chopped hazelnuts

Wash and drain the lettuce. Blanch for 5 minutes in lightly salted water. (If you have no stock, reserve the water, and add ½ stock cube to it.) Drain the lettuce well, pressing out as much moisture as possible, and chop them. Chop the onion finely. Melt the butter in a heavy pan and cook the chopped onions in it until they are transparent. Add the chopped lettuce and stir well until it is coated in butter. Cook for another 3—4 minutes, then pour on the heated stock. Simmer for 20 minutes, then put through the fine mesh of a vegetable mill or purée in the blender and return to the cleaned pan. Stir in the cream, taste for seasoning, reheat and serve with the chopped nuts sprinkled on top of the tureen or in individual bowls.

Serves 4—5.

MINESTRONE

½ cup dried haricot beans
1 large onion
1 large leek
½ pound tomatoes
2 stalks celery
1—2 carrots, depending on size
1 clove garlic
4 tablespoons olive oil
6 cups stock or water
2 ounces macaroni
salt and black pepper
1—2 tablespoons extra olive oil (optional)
1 cup grated Parmesan cheese
6 tablespoons chopped parsley (optional)

Rinse the beans and cover with 1—1½ cups of cold water. Cook very slowly in a small pan. When they begin to boil, remove from the heat and leave covered for 1 hour. Chop the vegetables. Heat 4 tablespoons of oil in a large pan, add the chopped vegetables and let them stew gently for 8—10 minutes. Heat the stock or water and pour over the vegetables. Add the beans with their cooking liquid. Bring to the boil and simmer gently until the beans are tender, about 1 hour. Add the macaroni and cook for another 15 minutes. Taste and adjust seasoning, adding black pepper to taste. For a strong olive oil flavor, add the extra spoonfuls now. Mix the grated cheese into the soup or serve it separately in a bowl, with another bowl of freshly chopped parsley.

Serves 8–10.

SOUPE AU PISTOU

1 onion
2 small leeks
2 small carrots
2 small zucchini
½ pound string beans
2 medium potatoes
½ pound fresh white haricot beans (1½ lb. in pod)
or
½ cup dried white haricots
½ cup olive oil
salt
2 ounces shell pasta or macaroni

Pistou:
4 cloves garlic
2 tomatoes
12 sprigs basil (fresh)
or
4 tablespoons chopped leaves
¼ cup olive oil
2 ounces grated Parmesan cheese

Dice the onion, leeks, carrots, zucchini, string beans and potatoes, keeping them in separate piles. Heat about 4 tablespoons of olive oil in a large heavy saucepan and cook the onion and leeks gently until they are pale golden. Pour in 5 cups boiling water and add the carrots and the haricot beans. (If using dried beans, they must be covered with cold water and pre-cooked until almost tender.) Bring back to a boil, add salt, cover and simmer for 45 minutes. Then add the potatoes, zucchini and string beans. Simmer for another 30 minutes. Add the pasta, and cook uncovered for 10 minutes more, or until pasta is just tender. Meanwhile prepare the *pistou.* Pound the garlic in a mortar. Cut the tomatoes, do not peel them, squeeze out the seeds and juice, and grill them until browned. Chop

the basil and add to the garlic in the mortar and pound again. After discarding the skins, add the chopped grilled tomatoes. Pound again until you have a fairly smooth paste, then add 4 tablespoons of olive oil drop-by-drop while stirring constantly. When the *pistou* is smooth and well mixed, pour it into the heated tureen, and add a ladleful of the boiling hot soup. Mix well, then add the rest gradually. Let stand for 5 minutes while the flavor develops. Serve the grated cheese separately.
  Serves 10.

PUMPKIN SOUP

2 pounds pumpkin
½ pound potatoes
½ pound tomatoes
1 large onion
4 cups chicken or vegetable stock
3 tablespoons butter
salt and black pepper
1 teaspoon chopped fresh basil, when available
or
4 tablespoons chopped parsley
¼ cup cream (optional)

Peel the pumpkin and cut in 2-inch cubes. Peel the potatoes and cut in similar sized pieces. Skin the tomatoes and chop coarsely. Put all three vegetables in a large pan with the stock. Bring to a boil and simmer, covered, for 15–20 minutes, until all are soft. Meanwhile chop the onion finely and stew gently in the butter until soft. When the mixed vegetables are cooked, push through the medium mesh of the vegetable mill (or use the blender, if you prefer), reserving about 1 cup of the liquid, or the soup may be too thin. Return the sieved soup to the cleaned pan and adjust the consistency by adding as much of the reserved liquid as is needed to make a soup like thin cream. Stir in the onion and its juices and add salt and black pepper to taste. Add the fresh basil if available; otherwise, add parsley. Stir in the cream, if used. (The cream makes a slightly richer and smoother soup.) Serve in bowls sprinkled with chopped parsley or fresh basil, if available.
  Serves 8.

A delicious and unusual soup, warm orange in color.

MIXED ROOT VEGETABLE SOUP

½ pound parsnips
½ pound carrots
½ pound turnips
4 tablespoons butter
6 cups beef stock
chopped parsley

Slice all the vegetables and sauté in the fat for 5 minutes, stirring now and then. Heat the stock in a large deep pan. When it is very hot, lift the sliced vegetables from the fat with a slotted spoon, and drop them into the stock. Simmer for 10 minutes, or until the vegetables are just tender, but not mushy. Put through the coarse mesh of a vegetable mill, reheat in the cleaned pan and season with salt and black pepper. Add plenty of chopped parsley or have a bowl of it on the table.
        Serves 8.

This is a good winter soup; it can also be made in the blender, although some of the coarse texture will be lost.

SOLFERINO SOUP

½ cup butter
1 onion
4 leeks
1½ pounds tomatoes
1½ pounds potatoes
1 clove garlic
10 cups chicken, veal
or
vegetable stock
¼ pound tiny carrots or diced large ones
salt and black pepper
2 tablespoons chopped parsley

Melt ¼ cup of the butter in a large, heavy saucepan and cook the sliced onion in it for 2–3 minutes. Slice the white part of the leeks, and add them to the onion, cooking gently until well softened, about 8 minutes. Peel and roughly chop the tomatoes, potatoes and garlic. Add to the pan. Add the heated stock, reserving a few spoonfuls, and simmer for 30 minutes. Slice the carrots thinly and cook separately in the reserved stock. When they are still slightly crisp, drain the liquid back into the soup and keep the carrots warm in a covered pan for a garnish. When the soup is cooked, put through the fine mesh of a vegetable mill or purée in the blender and return to the cleaned pan. Reheat, season carefully, add the remaining butter, the carrots and the chopped parsley, and serve.

Serves 10—12.

TOMATO AND CUCUMBER SOUP

1 cucumber
1 bunch spring onions
or
1 medium chopped onion
3 tablespoons butter
salt and black pepper
¾ pound tomatoes
lemon juice
cayenne
sugar
1 tablespoon sour cream

Slice the peeled cucumber and the onions. Melt the butter in a heavy pan and stew the sliced vegetables in it gently for about 5 minutes. (If you have to use a large onion, cook it alone for a few minutes in the butter before adding the cucumber.) Pour on 3 cups boiling water and simmer uncovered for 30 minutes. Season with salt and black pepper. Put the unpeeled tomatoes in a pan half full of boiling water. Cover and cook over medium heat for 10 minutes. Lift out the tomatoes and press them through the medium mesh of a vegetable mill. Discard the skins and pour the cucumber soup through the vegetable mill on top of the tomatoes. Mix well, season to taste with lemon juice, a little cayenne and a pinch of sugar, and more salt and black pepper if necessary. Stir in the sour cream. Serve hot or chilled. The freshness of the almost raw tomatoes makes a delicious contrast to the bland cucumber base.

Serves 4.

This soup freezes well.

TURNIP SOUP

1½ pounds turnips
4 tablespoons butter
2 cups light stock: chicken, veal or vegetable
2 cups milk or half-and-half
2 tablespoons chopped fresh chervil or parsley
salt and black pepper

Peel the turnips and slice them. Melt the butter and cook the sliced turnips in it slowly for 5 minutes. (If the turnips are very large, blanch them first by putting them, sliced, in a pan of cold water and bringing to a boil. Boil for 2 minutes, then drain and throw away the water.) After the turnips have cooked for 5 minutes in the butter pour on the heated stock. Simmer gently until the turnips are soft, about 20 minutes. Put the soup through the fine mesh of a vegetable mill together with the heated milk, or purée in a blender. Return to the cleaned pan and reheat, season with salt and black pepper, and serve sprinkled with chopped chervil or parsley.
Serves 4–6.

This soup freezes well.

WATERCRESS AND CUCUMBER SOUP

1 bunch watercress
1 cucumber
1 large potato
4 tablespoons butter
2 cups chicken stock
2 cups milk
salt and black pepper
4 tablespoons cream

Chop the watercress, stalks and all. Peel the cucumber and chop it. Peel the potato and slice it thinly. Melt the butter in a heavy pan and cook the watercress and cucumber gently for 4 minutes, stirring now and then. Add the sliced potato and stir until coated with fat and well mixed. Heat the stock and milk together and pour on. Season lightly with salt and simmer gently for 25 minutes. Cook slightly, push through the medium mesh of a vegetable mill and return to the cleaned pan. Reheat, adjust seasoning,

and stir in the cream. For a more elegant soup, reserve a few of the best leaves of the watercress. Put the soup in the blender instead of the vegetable mill and scatter the fresh leaves on top before serving.
    Serves 4—6.

This soup freezes well.

COLD AVOCADO SOUP

1 large avocado or 2 small ones
4 cups chicken stock
½ cup yoghurt
lemon juice
salt

Peel the avocado and remove the stone. Chop the flesh and put it in the blender with the cold stock. Blend till smooth, then add the yoghurt and blend again. Add lemon juice to taste and a pinch of salt. Chill for 2 hours before serving.
    Serves 4—5.

This beautiful pale green soup must not be made far in advance or both the color and the flavor will be lost.

BARLEY BROTH

7—8 cups beef stock
2 ounces pearl barley
salt and black pepper
½ pound carrots
1 pound leeks
½ pound turnips
¼ pound onions
¼ pound celery
½ cup chopped parsley

Heat the stock to boiling in a deep pot, skimming if necessary. Wash the barley well and put it into the boiling stock. Add salt. Dice the vegetables in equal sized pieces and add them to the stock. Simmer for 1 hour. Season to taste with salt and freshly ground black pepper. Serve with a good handful of freshly chopped parsley in each bowl.
    Serves 8—10.

CARROT AND TOMATO SOUP

¾ pounds carrots
¾ pounds tomatoes
4 tablespoons butter
4 cups chicken stock
1 cup milk and cream mixed
salt and black pepper
chopped parsley

Peel and slice the carrots; skin and chop the tomatoes. Melt the butter in a saucepan, put in the carrots and tomatoes and stew gently for 5 minutes. Heat the stock and add it to the saucepan. Bring to a boil and simmer until the carrots are very soft, about 35 minutes. Put through the medium mesh of the vegetable mill and return to the pan. Heat the milk and cream and stir into the soup. Add salt and black pepper to taste, and garnish with chopped parsley.
    Serves 6.

A smoother version can be made by putting the mixture in the blender with the milk and cream.

CAULIFLOWER SOUP

1 medium cauliflower
4 tablespoons butter
4 cups light chicken stock
4 tablespoons thin cream
salt and black pepper

Divide the cauliflower into sprigs and wash them well. Reserve one and chop the rest. Melt the butter in a saucepan and put in the chopped cauliflower. Cook gently in the butter for 5 minutes, stirring frequently. Heat the stock and pour it into the pan. Bring to a boil, cover and simmer for 20 minutes. Let the soup cool slightly, then purée it in the blender. Return to the cleaned pan and reheat. Taste for seasoning and stir in the cream. Serve in cups, either hot or chilled, with a little finely chopped raw cauliflower on top of each cup.
    Serves 4–5.

This soup freezes well.

CELERY CONSOMME

1 head celery
5 cups beef stock
salt and black pepper

Scrub the celery well, and chop it coarsely—leaves, root and all. Put in a pan with the cold stock and bring slowly to a boil. Simmer gently for 15–20 minutes, or until the stock is well flavored. Strain, return to the cleaned pan. Reheat and season with salt and black pepper. Serve hot with cheese straws.

Serves 4–6.

This delicate soup makes an ideal start to a rich meal.

LENTIL SOUP

1 pound brown (continental) lentils
1 onion
2 tablespoons olive oil
6 cups chicken, game or vegetable stock
1 stalk celery
1 carrot
2 cloves garlic
1 bay leaf
2 sprigs parsley
salt and black pepper

Pick over the lentils, wash and drain them well in a colander. Chop the onion and brown in the oil in a heavy pan. Add the lentils and stir frequently. Heat the stock and add to the lentils. Bring to a boil, lower the heat and add the sliced vegetables, herbs and seasonings. Simmer gently for 45–50 minutes, or until the lentils are soft, but unbroken. Adjust seasoning and serve as it is, or sieved if you prefer, or put half in the blender and mix the two halves together.

Serves 6–8.

MUSHROOM SOUP

½ pound mushrooms
4 cups chicken stock

½ cup yoghurt or sour cream
lemon juice

Chop the mushrooms. Heat the stock and add the mushrooms when it is almost boiling. Bring to a boil and simmer 15 minutes. Cool slightly, then purée in the blender. Add the yoghurt or sour cream, then blend again. Add lemon juice to taste, and salt and black pepper if needed. Serve hot with a little finely chopped parsley on top of each.
    Serves 4—5.

GREEN PEA SOUP

1 pound shelled peas
or
2 packages frozen peas
1 cup milk
1 cup thin cream
1 ounce butter (hot soup only)
a few fresh mint leaves (cold soup only)

Cook the peas in the minimum of lightly salted water, then put in the blender reserving 1 tablespoon whole peas for garnish. Add the milk and cream to the peas and blend again. Return to the cleaned pan and reheat, seasoning carefully with salt and black pepper. For a hot soup, add the butter and garnish with a few whole cooked peas in each cup. For a cold soup, omit the butter, chill for several hours or overnight, and garnish with chopped fresh mint.
    Serves 6.

SPLIT PEA SOUP

1 cup split peas
1 ham bone
2 medium onions
1 clove garlic (optional)
4 tablespoons olive oil
or
4 tablespoons butter
salt and black pepper

Cook the peas with the ham bone in 5 cups water until tender. Put aside. Chop the onions and cook in the oil (or butter) until soft and golden, adding the garlic halfway through. Throw away the ham bone and mix the onions into the soup. Reheat, seasoning with salt and black pepper.

Serves 6.

POTATO AND ONION SOUP

2 large onions
6 tablespoons butter
2 large potatoes
2½ cups chicken stock
2½ cups creamy milk or milk and cream mixed
salt and black pepper

Chop the onions and cook in the butter until transparent. Peel the potatoes, halve them, and slice each half thinly. Add them to the onions and stir around for a minute or two until coated with fat and well mixed. Heat the stock and pour over the mixture. Season with salt and pepper and simmer until the potatoes are soft, about 20—30 minutes. Heat the milk and stir it in. Mix well, taste and adjust seasoning. Serve as it is, or put through medium mesh of a vegetable mill, or purée in the blender, according to your taste. If made into a smooth soup, it should have a garnish of chopped parsley sprinkled on top.

Serves 6

PROVENÇAL SOUP

1 pound potatoes
1 pound tomatoes
½ pound onions
1 clove garlic
5 cups stock
2 pounds green peas in pods
or
½ pound frozen petits pois
3 tablespoons butter
salt and black pepper

Peel the potatoes and cut them in quarters. Skin the tomatoes and cut in quarters. Slice the onions and crush the garlic. Shell the peas. Put the potatoes, tomatoes, onions and garlic in a pan with the stock. Bring to a boil and simmer slowly for 1½ hours. Put through the medium mesh of a vegetable mill and return to the cleaned pan. Cook the peas separately and add to the reheated soup. Adjust seasoning and serve.

Serves 6.

SORREL SOUP

½ pound sorrel
or
sorrel, spinach and lettuce, mixed
4 tablespoons butter
3 cups chicken stock
salt and black pepper
½ cup cream
2 egg yolks

Wash and dry the greens. Heat the butter in a heavy pan, put in the greens and cook gently for 6 minutes. Heat the stock and pour into pan. Bring to simmering point, add a little salt and cover the pan. Simmer for 25 minutes. Put through the medium mesh of the vegetable mill. Return to the cleaned pan and reheat. Add salt and black pepper to taste. Beat the egg yolks with the cream, stir in a ladleful of the hot soup, then return the mixture to the pan. Reheat without allowing to boil.

Serves 4.

COLD SPINACH SOUP

1 package frozen chopped spinach
1 cup sour cream
½ cup canned vichyssoise
approximately ½ cup buttermilk
juice of 1 lemon
1 tablespoon catsup
few drops Tabasco sauce

Cook the frozen spinach and squeeze out as much moisture as possible. Mix the sour cream with the vichyssoise, beat in the spinach, and thin to slightly more than the desired consistency with buttermilk. (This soup will become thicker when chilled.) Flavor with lemon juice to taste, and add the catsup and Tabasco sauce. Chill for several hours before serving.
Serves 4—5

SPRING VEGETABLE SOUP

½ pound young carrots
½ pound young turnips
2 small leeks
1 stalk celery
6 tablespoons butter or olive oil
7 cups light stock: chicken, veal or vegetable
½ pound shelled peas (about 2 pounds in the pod)
salt and black pepper

Chop the carrots, turnips, leeks and celery and stew them very gently in the butter or oil in a covered pot for 10—15 minutes. Heat 6 cups of the stock and add to the pan. Simmer gently for 30 minutes. Meanwhile cook the peas in the remaining cup of stock until soft, and purée in the blender. When the mixed vegetables are cooked, stir in the purée of green peas, reheat, season lightly, and serve.
Serves 6—8.

TOMATO CONSOMME

6 tomatoes
1 head celery
2 leeks
1 carrot
2 egg whites
5 cups beef stock
¾ pound ground beef
2 tablespoons lemon juice
1 teaspoon sugar

salt and black pepper
4 tablespoons whipped cream
or
sour cream
or
croutons (optional)

Chop the vegetables and beat the egg whites until stiff. Put them all in a large pan with the stock and the ground beef. Bring slowly to a boil and simmer for 1 hour. Strain through a muslin cloth. Reheat in the cleaned pan and add lemon juice, sugar, salt and pepper to taste. Serve in individual cups, either plain or with a spoon of whipped or sour cream, or a few croutons in each cup.

Serves 6.

TERRY'S TOMATO SOUP

1 medium onion
4 tablespoons butter
1½ pounds tomatoes
2½ cups light stock: chicken, veal or vegetable
salt and black pepper and sugar
2 tablespoons chopped chervil, basil, chives
or
parsley as available

Chop the onion finely and cook it gently in the butter until soft. Add the peeled and roughly chopped tomatoes. After a few minutes softening in the butter, stirring now and then, pour on the heated stock. Season with salt, black pepper and a pinch of sugar. Simmer for 20 minutes. Pass through the medium mesh of a vegetable mill. Serve in individual cups, sprinkling each one with finely chopped fresh basil, chervil, chives or parsley, as available.

Serves 4.

A VEGETABLE CONSOMME

1 pound leeks
½ pound carrots
1 red or green pepper
½ celeriac or ½ head celery

½ pound tomatoes
3–4 sprigs parsley
salt and black pepper
lemon juice

Clean the carrots and leeks and slice finely. Chop the pepper, removing the seeds. Peel the celeriac, or scrub the celery, including leaves and chop. Coarsely chop the unpeeled tomatoes. Put all the vegetables with the parsley in a deep pot with 5 cups cold water. Bring slowly to a boil and simmer for 2–3 hours. Pour through a strainer, return to the cleaned pan, reheat and season with salt, black pepper and a little lemon juice.
    Serves 4–6.

Serve hot or chilled.

WATERCRESS AND BEAN SPROUT SOUP

5 cups duck or chicken stock
1 bunch watercress, chopped (2 cups)
½ pound bean sprouts
lemon juice
soy sauce
salt and black pepper

Heat the stock until almost boiling, then add the watercress. Simmer for 2 minutes, then add the bean sprouts. Simmer for 3 more minutes, add lemon juice, a dash of soy sauce, salt and black pepper to taste, and serve.
    Serves 6.

VICHYSSOISE

3 tablespoons butter
4 good-sized leeks
1 onion
5 cups chicken stock
2 sprigs parsley
1 celery stalk
2 medium potatoes
salt and black pepper
½ cup thick cream
12 tablespoons chopped chives

Chop the leeks and the onion, and slice the potato thinly. Melt the butter in a heavy pan, put in the leeks and the onion, and cook gently until golden and soft. Add the potatoes and stir until coated with butter. Pour in the heated stock, add the parsley and celery, season with salt and black pepper, and simmer until the potatoes are soft, about 20–30 minutes. Put the soup in the blender after it has cooled slightly, and pour in the cream. Chill for at least 12 hours before serving. (This soup is better made the day before.) Serve in chilled cups sprinkled with chopped chives.

Serves 8.

[3]

Pastry and Breads

PIROG

Dough:
3½ cups flour
¾ ounce yeast
½ cup tepid water
3 egg yolks
salt
pinch of sugar
½ cup tepid milk
1 cup butter

Filling I:
heart of a green cabbage
2 hard-boiled eggs
2 tablespoons butter
salt and black pepper

Filling II:
½ pound young carrots
2 hard-boiled eggs
2 tablespoons butter
salt and black pepper

Filling III:
½ pound mushrooms
2 hard-boiled eggs
4 tablespoons butter
salt and black pepper

To make the dough, sift the flour with a pinch of salt into a large warmed bowl. Put the yeast and the sugar into a cup with the tepid water. Leave this in a warm place for 10 minutes, until it starts to bubble. Beat the eggs into the milk. Cream the butter. Make a well in the center of the flour, pour in the yeast mixture and cover it with the rest of the flour. Add the egg and milk mixture, and stir till blended. Beat in the creamed butter and turn onto a floured board and knead briefly. Return to the bowl and cover with a floured cloth. Leave in a warm place for 2 hours, by which time it should have doubled in bulk. Punch down, turn out, and knead again briefly. Roll out into a large oval on a floured baking sheet.

To make the filling: Filling I. Cut the heart of the green cabbage in half and cook until just tender in boiling salted water, drain very well and chop. Melt the butter in a saucepan, toss the cabbage in it, add the chopped eggs, and season quite highly with salt and freshly ground black pepper.
Filling II. Cook the carrots, whole or in halves according to size, in boiling salted water until tender. Drain well and chop them. Melt the butter in a saucepan, toss the carrots in it, and the chopped eggs and season well with salt and black pepper.
Filling III. Slice the mushrooms and cook gently in a covered sauté pan in the butter. When soft, add the chopped eggs and mix. Season with salt and black pepper.

To assemble: Put the filling on one half of the oval and cover with the other half. Pinch the edges together, sealing with a little beaten egg. Allow to rise in the same warm place for 15—20 minutes. Bake in the oven for 20 minutes at 400 degrees. Lay on a cutting board and cut in thick slices. This makes a delicious bread with a vegetable filling.
        Serves 8 as a first course.

PIZZA

Dough:
2 cups white flour
1½ teaspoons sea salt
½ ounce yeast

Filling:
1 pound onions
4—5 tablespoons olive oil
1½ pounds tomatoes
6 ounces Mozarella
or
other Italian cheese
1 clove garlic
1 tablespoon chopped fresh basil
or
marjoram or combination
salt and black pepper
8 anchovy fillets
or
12 black olives, pits removed, or 12 slices pepperoni

To make the dough, sift the flour. Put the yeast in a cup with 2 tablespoons of warm water and leave in a warm place for 10 minutes. Stir into a well in the flour, then mix in approximately ½ cup tepid water. Turn out and knead until smooth and elastic, about 4 minutes. Put on a plate and cover with a floured cloth in a warm place for 2 hours, until doubled in size. To make the filling, chop the onions and stew them gently in oil in a covered pan for 30 minutes. Drain off all the oil and season with salt and pepper. Skin the tomatoes and chop coarsely. Cook briskly in a little oil until softened and most of the juice has evaporated—about 12—15 minutes. Roll and press out the dough into a large circle between 1/4 and 1/8 inch thick, leaving a thicker rim round the edge to enclose the filling. Place on a greased baking sheet. Cover the dough with the onions, then add the thinly sliced cheese and the tomatoes. Mince or crush the garlic and scatter over the tomatoes with the basil, salt and black pepper. Lay the anchovy fillets, olives or the sliced sausage over the top. Put the pizza in the oven heated to 400 degrees, turn down immediately to 350 degrees, and cook for about 25 minutes, until golden.
    Serves 6.

There are endless variations of fillings for pizza; one alternative is to omit the onions, increase the tomatoes, and lay the sliced cheese over the tomatoes, leaving out anchovies, etc.

GREEN GNOCCHI

½ pound cooked spinach
salt and black pepper
nutmeg
2 tablespoons butter
6 ounces ricotta cheese
1 ounce grated Fontina or Parmesan cheese
2 eggs
2½ tablespoons flour
4 tablespoons grated Parmesan cheese

Chop the spinach finely and put through the medium mesh of a vegetable mill. Return the puree to the cleaned pan and stir over gentle heat until well dried. Stir in the butter, salt, black pepper and a grating of nutmeg. When all is smooth and hot, stir in the mashed ricotta cheese. Stir again until smooth, then shake in the Fontina or Parmesan cheese. Stir again till smooth and melted, then remove from the fire and stir in the beaten eggs and the flour. Pour the mixture into a shallow dish and leave to cool. When cold, place in the refrigerator overnight, or even longer—this can be left in the refrigerator for 2–3 days without harm. Do not cover the dish. When ready to serve, take large teaspoons of the mixture with two floured spoons, and roll on a floured board into oval shapes. Bring a large pan of very lightly salted water to a boil, reduce to a gentle simmer, and drop in a batch of the gnocchi. Simmer gently all the time, watching them carefully. After 5 minutes lift them out with a slotted spoon and drain. Place them in a heated shallow dish in a warm place while you cook the rest of the gnocchi. They can be sprinkled with grated cheese and melted butter and broiled briefly, or served simply with Parmesan, grated, and passed separately.
    Serves 3–4.

HERB DUMPLINGS

1 cup all-purpose flour
2 teaspoons baking powder
salt
2 tablespoons butter
1 egg

about 1/8 cup milk
3 tablespoons finely chopped fresh herbs:
chervil, dill, parsley

Sift the flour with baking powder and a pinch of salt. Cut the butter in small pieces and rub into the flour. Beat the egg and add milk, up to 3 fluid ounces. Add the chopped herbs to the egg and milk and pour onto the flour mixture gradually, mixing with the blade of a knife. Stop as soon as the mixture becomes clinging and soft. Add more milk by drops if still too dry. Using two large teaspoons, take small scoops of the mixture and drop onto the surface of the casserole, about 15 minutes before serving. Makes about 12 dumplings.
    Serves 6.

QUICHE OF HERBS AND CHEESE

short pastry (see page 37)
1 small head romaine lettuce
1 bunch watercress
¼ pound spinach
¼ pound sorrel, when available
1 bunch parsley
½ pound Brie cheese
1 cup thin cream
2 eggs
black pepper

Follow usual procedure for pre-baking pastry in a quiche or pie pan. Put all the greens into a large pan of boiling water for 5 minutes, then drain. Press in a colander to extract as much moisture as possible. Turn them onto a board and chop roughly, in pieces about ½-inch square. Cut the rind off the cheese and chop the firm parts. Put it in a bowl in a very low oven (200 degrees) with half the cream until melted, 10–15 minutes. Put in the blender or through a sieve to make it smooth. Beat the eggs into the rest of the cream and combine with the cheese mixture. Scatter the chopped greens in the pastry case and pour the cheese mixture over. Sprinkle with pepper and bake at 350 degrees for 30 minutes.
    Serves 6.

ONION SHORTCAKE

1 cup flour
1 teaspoon baking powder
¼ teaspoon salt
2 tablespoons butter
about 6 tablespoons milk
1 pound onions
5 tablespoons butter
salt and black pepper
1 egg
½ cup cream

Sift the flour with the salt and baking powder. Cut 2 tablespoons butter in small pieces and rub into the flour, or cut in with a fork. Mix with enough milk to make a dough. Turn onto a floured board and knead once or twice. Put aside while you make the onion mixture. Slice the onions thinly and evenly. Melt the remaining butter in a heavy frying pan and cook the onions gently until they are soft. Stir now and then so that they do not stick. Beat the egg with the cream; season with salt and black pepper. When the onions are soft, lift them out of the pan with a slotted spoon, leaving behind the juice. Put them into a bowl and beat in the egg and cream mixture. Taste for seasoning and adjust. Roll and pat out the shortcake till ¼ inch thick. Place in a quiche or a pie dish. Pour the onion mixture in and cook for 25 minutes at 425 degrees. Serve hot or warm.
    Serves 4.

ZUCCHINI QUICHE

short pastry (see page 37)
1 pound zucchini
2 eggs
½ cup thick cream
salt and black pepper
nutmeg

To make the filling, cut the zucchini in ½-inch slices and cook in boiling salted water for 12 minutes. Drain, pressing out excess moisture with the back of a wooden spoon. Beat two eggs with the cream and season well with salt, black pepper and nutmeg. Pour over the zucchini, mix lightly, and pour into the pre-baked pastry. Bake for 30 minutes at 350 degrees.

Serves 5–6.

ONION AND BACON QUICHE

short pastry (see page 37)
1 egg yolk, beaten
1½ pounds onions
2–3 slices bacon
6 tablespoons butter
2 eggs
½ cup cream
salt and black pepper

Line a 10-inch quiche or pie pan with the pastry, brush with beaten egg yolk and pre-bake for 10 minutes at 400 degrees. Slice the onions and cook in the butter until soft. Chop the bacon and add it to the onions. When all is golden, remove from the fire. Beat the eggs with the cream and add salt and black pepper. Mix with the onions and bacon and taste for seasoning. Pour into the pie pan and bake for 30 minutes at 400 degrees.

Serves 6.

The bacon can be omitted if preferred.

POTATO AND HERB PIE

1½ pounds short pastry (see page 37)
1 pound new potatoes
4 tablespoons butter
salt and black pepper and nutmeg
4 tablespoons chopped fresh herbs:
chervil, chives, parsley, dill
1 egg yolk
½ cup thick cream

Roll out half the pastry and line a quiche pan. Slice the peeled potatoes thinly and evenly. Arrange in layers in the pastry, dotting each layer with butter, seasoning with salt, black pepper and grated nutmeg. Cover with aluminum foil brushed with beaten egg yolk. Bake for 1 hour at 350 degrees. Heat the cream, season with salt and black pepper and stir in the herbs. Remove the foil and pour the cream over the potatoes. Replace the foil and bake for 5 minutes more.

Serves 6.

TOMATO AND MUSTARD QUICHE

short pastry (see page 37)
1 egg yolk
1–2 tablespoons mustard
1 pound tomatoes
4 eggs
1 cup thick cream
salt and black pepper
2 ounces grated Gruyère cheese

Line a 10-inch quiche pan with the pastry, brush with the beaten egg yolk, prick the bottom with a fork and prebake for 10 minutes at 400 degrees. When it has cooled, spread a thin layer of mustard over the bottom. Skin the tomatoes and chop coarsely, discarding seeds and juice. Beat the eggs, add the cream and season carefully with salt and black pepper. Stir in the tomatoes and the cheese, keeping back a handful of cheese. Pour into the quiche pan and scatter the reserved cheese over the top. Bake at 325 degrees until golden and puffed up, 35–40 minutes. Serve immediately.

Serves 6.

SPINACH AND TOMATO QUICHE

cheese pastry (see page 37)
1 pound spinach
½ pound onions
¾ pound tomatoes
6 tablespoons butter
1 clove garlic
salt and black pepper
2 eggs
½ cup thin cream

Line a 10-inch quiche pan with the pastry (ordinary short pastry can be substituted for the cheese pastry), brush with beaten egg yolk and pre-bake for 10 minutes at 400 degrees. Clean and chop the spinach and cook in half the butter until softened. Chop the onions and cook in half the remaining butter until soft and golden. Peel and chop the tomatoes; cook them in the remaining butter until softened, 4–6 minutes. Mix the tomatoes and the onions together, add the crushed garlic and season with salt and black pepper. Spread half the mixture over the bottom of the pastry, put the spinach over it, and cover with the remaining tomato and onion. Beat the eggs and the cream and pour over the top. Bake for 30 minutes at 375 degrees.

Serves 6.

An excellent dish which can be kept and eaten when still warm, or the next day when cold. A perfect dish to take on a picnic.

CHEESE PASTRY

2 cups all-purpose flour
salt
1¼ cups grated Cheddar cheese
6 tablespoons very cold butter
about ½ cup iced water

Sift the flour into a large bowl with salt. Mix in the grated cheese with the blade of a knife. Cut the butter into the bowl. Rub in very quickly with the finger tips. Add just enough iced water to hold dough together. Make into a ball and chill for 30 minutes. Roll out and line a 9–10 inch quiche pan.

This makes an unusual and excellent pastry for vegetable quiches. It can be used for any vegetable or mixture of vegetables, only remember to omit any other cheese that occurs in the recipe.

SHORT PASTRY

2 cups all-purpose flour
¾ cup very cold butter
1 egg yolk (optional)
pinch salt
4–8 tablespoons iced water

Sift the flour into a large bowl. Add the salt. Cut the butter into small bits and rub into the flour. Stir in the egg yolk, and add enough iced water to make the mixture hold together. Form into a ball, and chill for 30 minutes or longer. This makes enough pastry to line a 10-inch quiche or pie pan. The egg yolk is optional, but it gives a richer pastry.

[4]

Egg Dishes

EGGS WITH WATERCRESS SAUCE
---

8 eggs
2 large slices stale bread
approximately 2 tablespoons butter
1 clove garlic

Watercress sauce:
1 cup chicken stock
1 tablespoon butter
1 tablespoon flour
¼ cup cream, or more according to taste
salt and black pepper

Poach the eggs or boil for exactly 5 minutes. If boiled, shell them as soon as they are cool enough to handle. Remove the crusts from the bread and cut each slice in 4 triangles. Heat 2 tablespoons butter and fry the croutons until golden on each side. Cut the clove of garlic in half, score each cut surface with a knife, and rub the fried bread on each side with it. Keep warm while you make the sauce. Chop the watercress and simmer in the stock for 5 minutes. Pour the contents of the pan into the blender or push through the fine mesh of the vegetable mill. Melt the butter, stir in the flour and cook for

2—3 minutes, stirring constantly. Pour in the blended watercress and stock and stir till smooth. Simmer gently for a few minutes, then add the cream. Season with salt and black pepper. Lay the eggs in a shallow dish and pour the sauce over them. Surround with the croutons.
  Serves 4—6.

VEGETABLE CURRY

1 cauliflower
½ pound tiny carrots
½ pound small zucchini
½ pound Jerusalem artichokes (optional)
½ pound string beans
½ pound lima beans or peas

Curry sauce:
3 tablespoons butter
2½ tablespoons flour
1½ tablespoons curry powder
1 cup thin cream
approximately 2 tablespoons sweet fruit juice
or
juice from sweet pickle
4 hard-boiled eggs

Divide the cauliflower into sprigs, leave the carrots whole, slice the un-peeled zucchini in ¾-inch slices, slice the artichokes likewise, cut the beans in 1-inch chunks. Cook each separately in the minimum of lightly salted water, reserving it afterwards, while you keep the vegetables hot. To make the sauce, melt the butter, stir in the flour and cook for 3 minutes, adding the curry powder halfway through. Measure 2½ cups of the vegetable stock, heat it, and blend with the *roux*. Stir until smooth and simmer for 3 minutes. Add the cream and blend again, then the fruit or pickle juice. When all is smooth and well mixed, pour over the vegetables in a serving bowl and mix. Cut the hard-boiled eggs into chunks and scatter them over the top.
  Serves 6.

Best made a day in advance and reheated; this curry is also good cold. Serve alone, or with boiled rice for a more substantial dish.

LENTILS WITH HARD-BOILED EGGS

2 ounces beef drippings
1 onion
2 carrots
1 stalk celery
1 pound brown lentils
1 clove garlic
Stock: beef, duck or game
½ pound piece bacon or ham bone
black pepper
6 hard-boiled eggs

Melt the drippings in a heavy pan. Chop the onion and cook in the fat until golden. Add the sliced carrots and the diced celery. Stir around for a few minutes, then add the lentils, washed but not soaked. When they are well coated with fat, add the minced garlic and pour on enough stock almost to cover them. Put in the bacon and season with black pepper. Simmer gently for 45 minutes. When the lentils are soft, the liquid should have almost boiled away. Pour into a serving dish and lay the halved hard-boiled eggs on top. Throw away the bacon, unless it is a nice piece, in which case cut it in slices and lay on top with the eggs.

Serves 4–6.

STUFFED EGGS REMOULADE

6 eggs
1 head celery

Sauce rémoulade:
1 egg yolk
salt and black pepper
1 heaped teaspoon Dijon mustard
1 tablespoon white wine vinegar
1 tablespoon tarragon vinegar
½ cup olive oil
2 tablespoons sour cream (optional)

Boil the eggs for 12 minutes, then cool in a bowl of cold water. When cold, remove the shells and cut them in half. Take out the yolks and reserve them.

Scrub the celery and chop finely, reserving the best leaves for a garnish. Make the sauce: mash one of the reserved egg yolks in a bowl, and beat in the raw yolk to form a smooth paste. Add a pinch of salt and black pepper. Beat in the mustard and add the vinegar very gradually. Then add the oil drop by drop, as for mayonnaise. When finished, taste for seasoning and add the sour cream. Mix the chopped celery with the sauce and spoon into the egg whites. (Two or three of the hard-boiled egg yolks can be chopped and added to the mixture, or they can be used for another dish.) Garnish the stuffed eggs with the celery leaves.

Serves 4.

STUFFED EGGS GUACAMOLE

---

6 eggs

Guacamole
1 large avocado
2 tomatoes
4 scallions or ½ small onion
1 small green pepper
1 green chili pepper
salt and black pepper
1 tablespoon lemon juice
1 tablespoon olive oil
4–6 large lettuce leaves

Cook the eggs for 12 minutes in boiling water, and cool in a bowl of cold water. Make the guacamole: peel the avocado and remove the stone. Cut the flesh into small dice. Skin the tomatoes and chop them also, discarding the seeds and juice. Chop the spring onions and the pepper, discarding all the seeds. Pour boiling water over the chili pepper and leave for 2 minutes, then drain and chop finely, avoiding all the seeds. Mix all together, seasoning with salt and black pepper. Stir in the lemon juice and olive oil. Cut the shelled eggs in half and remove the yolks. Chop 2 or 3 of them and stir into the guacamole. Spoon the mixture into the egg whites and arrange on a bed of lettuce leaves.

Serves 4.

EGGS SARDOU

6 artichoke bottoms
2½ pounds fresh spinach
or
1 pound frozen chopped spinach
2 tablespoons butter
1 tablespoon flour
salt and black pepper
2 tablespoons cream
6 poached eggs
sauce hollandaise (see p. 130)

Cook the artichoke bottoms (see p. 148) and keep hot. Make a well-seasoned spinach purée by cooking the fresh spinach, chopping and putting through the fine mesh of a vegetable mill. Return to the cleaned pan and dry out as much as possible over gentle heat. (If using frozen chopped spinach, simply cook as usual, then dry out as above.) Melt the butter, stir in the flour and cook for 1 minute. Stir in the spinach purée and simmer for 3 minutes. Season well with salt, black pepper and grated nutmeg. Add the cream. Have the poached eggs well drained and still hot. Make the *sauce hollandaise*. Place the artichoke bottoms on a flat dish, divide the spinach purée among them, and lay an egg on each. Cover with *sauce hollandaise* and serve immediately.

Serves 6.

This dish takes a lot of work, so do not try to do anything else at the same time.

POACHED EGGS ON SPINACH PUREE

2½ pounds fresh spinach
or
1 pound frozen chopped spinach
2 tablespoons butter
2 teaspoons flour
salt and black pepper
nutmeg
4 eggs
cream sauce (see p. 134)

Cook the spinach and drain well. Chop and push through the fine mesh of a vegetable mill. (If using frozen chopped spinach, cook according to directions on the package, and dry out as much moisture as possible.) Melt the butter, stir in the flour, and add the spinach purée. Cook till smooth, and simmer for 4 minutes, stirring often. Season with salt, black pepper and a little grated nutmeg. Poach the eggs and lay on a cloth to drain. (You also can use eggs boiled for exactly 5 minutes, cooled and shelled.) Keep the eggs warm while you make the cream sauce. Put the eggs in a shallow dish, pour in the spinach purée, and spoon a little sauce over each egg. Pass the rest of the sauce separately.

Serves 4.

EGGPLANT OMELETTE

1 medium eggplant
4 eggs
about 1 tablespoon olive oil
salt and black pepper
about 1 tablespoon butter

Peel the eggplant, cut in ¼-inch slices, then cut each slice in thin strips. Salt the strips and leave for 30 minutes. Squeeze the eggplant dry in a cloth. Heat enough oil to cover the bottom of the frying pan, and cook the strips until soft and golden. Drain on paper towels. Keep warm. Beat the eggs, season with salt and black pepper, and make an omelette. When almost set, sprinkle the eggplant in an even layer across one half of the omelette, fold it over and turn onto a heated platter. Serve immediately.

Serves 2.

SWEET PEPPER OMELETTE

1 small red pepper
1 small green pepper
1 tablespoon olive oil or butter
4 eggs
salt and black pepper
1 tablespoon butter

Skin the peppers by placing them under a hot grill and turning until blackened on all sides. When cool, remove all the skin and cut the flesh in thin strips after removing all the seeds. Soften for 2 minutes in a little butter or oil before adding to the omelette. Beat the eggs, season with salt and black pepper, and make an omelette with the butter. When almost set, sprinkle the strips of pepper in an even layer across one half of the omelette, and fold it over onto a hot dish. Serve immediately.

Serves 2.

SCRAMBLED EGGS WITH SWEET CORN

4 ears fresh corn
or
1 package frozen corn
or
1 14-ounce can kernel corn
4 strips bacon
2 tablespoons butter
6 eggs
salt and black pepper

If using fresh corn, cut the kernels off the cobs with a sharp knife, and scrape all the juice as well. Simmer in a very little lightly salted water till tender, about 5 minutes. Drain. Otherwise, prepare the corn according to the directions on the package. Chop the bacon. Fry the bacon in the butter until golden. Add the cooked corn and stir over moderate heat until heated. Season with salt and black pepper. Beat the eggs and pour onto the corn. Stir constantly with a wooden spoon until hot and well mixed.

Serves 3–4.

PIPERADE

1 Spanish onion
1 green pepper
1 red pepper
4 large tomatoes
4 tablespoons olive oil
2 cloves garlic
salt and black pepper
5 eggs

Chop the onion; cut the peppers in strips, discarding seeds and inner white part; skin and chop the tomatoes; mince the garlic. Heat the oil in a sauté pan and cook the onion until it starts to soften and color. Add the peppers and cook for 10 minutes over a low flame. Add the tomatoes and the garlic and cook another 10 minutes. Season with salt and black pepper. Beat the eggs lightly and pour into the *piperade*. Cook for 2–3 minutes, stirring now and then, until the eggs have thickened like lightly scrambled eggs. Serve immediately.

Serves 3–4.

SCRAMBLED EGGS WITH MUSHROOMS

6 ounces mushrooms
4 tablespoons butter
8 eggs
salt and black pepper

Slice the mushrooms and cook in half the butter until soft. Drain them and keep hot. Scramble the eggs in the remaining butter, seasoning well with salt and black pepper. When they are almost set, stir in the mushrooms and cook a few moments longer. Garnish with croutons of bread fried in butter.

Serves 4.

SCRAMBLED EGGS WITH RED PEPPERS

1 large red pepper
3 tablespoons butter
1 tablespoon oil
8 eggs
salt and black pepper

Skin the pepper by placing it under a hot grill and turning until the skin is blackened. Remove with a knife. Cut the pepper in strips, discarding the pith and seeds. Heat 1 tablespoon butter and the oil in a frying pan and cook the pepper for about 3 minutes, until softened. Beat the eggs with salt and black pepper and scramble in the remaining butter. About halfway through the cooking, add the pepper and mix well with the eggs as they finish cooking.

Serves 4.

SCRAMBLED EGGS WITH TOMATOES

½ pound tomatoes
4 tablespoons butter
8 eggs
salt and black pepper
1–2 teaspoons chopped, fresh basil (optional)
sugar

Peel the tomatoes and chop them, discarding seeds and juice. Cook gently in half the butter for a few minutes, until softened. Season with a little salt and black pepper and a pinch of sugar, adding the basil to taste. Scramble the eggs as usual in the remaining butter, adding the tomatoes when the eggs are about three-quarters cooked. Serve garnished with croutons of bread fried in butter.

Serves 4.

EGGS ST. GERMAIN

1 pound shelled peas
(about 3½ pounds peas in the pod)
1¼ cups chicken stock
2 tablespoons cream
2 tablespoons butter
salt and black pepper
4 eggs
cream sauce (see page 134)

Cook the peas in the stock until soft. Drain and reserve the stock. Put the peas in the blender with ½ cup of the stock. Return the purée to the cleaned pan and stir in the butter, cut in small bits, over a gentle heat. Add the cream. Season to taste. Boil the eggs for 5 minutes, cool and shell. Make the cream sauce using the remaining stock. Put the eggs in a shallow dish and pour pea purée over them. Spoon a little of the sauce over each egg, and pass the rest separately.

Serves 4.

[5]

Fritters and Pancakes

Batter I (French):
1 cup all-purpose flour
salt
2 tablespoons arachide oil
½ cup tepid water
1 egg white, stiffly beaten

Sift the flour with a pinch of salt. Stir in the oil, then mix in the tepid water until you have the consistency of thick cream. (You may need slightly more than ½ cup.) Leave for about 2 hours in a cool place. Just before using, beat again, and fold in the stiffly beaten egg white. This makes an excellent light batter, suitable for all types of fritters.

Batter II (Japanese tempura):
1 egg
½ cup iced water
1 cup flour

Beat the egg, stir in the iced water and the sifted flour. Use immediately. This mixture gives a golden coating to the food, familiar to all those who eat in Oriental restaurants.

Batter III (American):
¾ cup flour
salt
1 egg
½ cup flat beer

Sift the flour with a pinch of salt. Make a well in the middle and break in the egg. Mix the egg and the flour with a whisk, stirring in the beer gradually at the same time, until all are mixed into a smooth batter. Let stand for about 2 hours if possible, before using. If preferred, the egg can be separated, and the white folded in at the last moment. A good all-purpose batter.

FRITTO MISTO OF VEGETABLES

2 tomatoes
2 zucchini
2 small onions
or
2 small beets, already cooked
½ cucumber
1 small eggplant
or
1 small eggplant
2 zucchini
2 tomatoes

fritter batter
2 lemons (optional)

Choose a selection of vegetables that make a color contrast, and prepare them as follows: cut the unpeeled tomatoes and zucchini in thin slices, the tomatoes vertically, the zucchini diagonally. Peel the onions and slice thinly, being careful not to divide up the slices into rings. Peel the cooked beets and slice equally thinly; slice the unpeeled cucumber and eggplant in similar fashion. Keep the vegetables separate, and dip each batch in batter, using tongs to lift them out and scraping off excess batter on the edge of the bowl. (If using beets, do them last of all as they color the batter.) Have a pan of deep oil heated to about 360 degrees and drop in the slices in small batches. Flip each slice once, and as soon as it is golden and puffed up on both sides, lift out and drain on soft paper. When all pieces are cooked, arrange them on a hot platter, or make a mixture of vegetables in individual dishes. Serve with quartered lemons, or skordalia (see p. 132).

Serves 4.

CELERIAC CROQUETTES

1 celeriac, approximately ¾ pound
¾ pound potatoes
2 egg yolks
1 whole egg
2 tablespoons butter
salt and black pepper
dry breadcrumbs

Cut the celeriac into pieces and cook in boiling salted water till tender, about 20–30 minutes. Peel the potatoes and cook separately. Dry out both celeriac and potatoes as much as possible, then push each one through the medium mesh of the vegetable mill or purée in a blender. Mix the two purées and return to the cleaned pan. Dry out again as much as possible stirring over a low flame. Beat in the butter, and season with salt and black pepper. If the purée still seems slightly moist, stir in ½ tablespoon flour. Off the flame stir in the egg yolks and mix well. Pour into a shallow dish, cover with a greased piece of saran wrap, and put in the refrigerator for several hours, or overnight. (This makes the purée drier, and easier to handle.) The next day, divide into equal sized pieces, form into rolls like corks, and dip first in beaten egg and then in the white breadcrumbs. Fry in a mixture of butter and oil or deep fry, if preferred. Serve immediately. Fried parsley makes a nice garnish if the croquettes are to be eaten on their own. Good served with a tomato sauce. Makes 16–18 croquettes.

Serves 6.

BRUSSELS SPROUTS IN BATTER

½ pound Brussels sprouts
fritter batter

Throw the sprouts into boiling salted water and cook briskly until almost tender, about 5 minutes. Drain well, and pat dry in a cloth. Dip each one in fritter batter and drop into deep fat or oil heated to about 360 degrees. Cook until they rise to the surface, and are golden brown and soft in the center. Drain on paper towels and serve with a tomato sauce (see page 142).

Serves 4.

EGGPLANT FRITTERS

½ pound eggplant
fritter batter
2 lemons (optional)

Halve the eggplant, then slice it. Sprinkle with salt and leave to drain for 30 minutes. Rinse and dry the slices and dip them in the batter. Lift them out with tongs, scraping off excess batter. Drop them into oil heated to about 360 degrees, a few at a time, and cook for about 3–4 minutes. Turn them over halfway through with a slotted spoon. Drain on paper towels and keep warm while you fry the next batch. Serve with skordalia, a spicy tomato sauce, or halved lemons.

Serves 4.

Do not try to make this dish for more than 3–4 people, as everything must be prepared at the last minute.

CORN FRITTERS

1 cup corn kernels,
cut off the cob (about 2–3 cobs)
4 tablespoons thick cream
2 tablespoons flour
½ teaspoon baking powder
½ teaspoon salt
black pepper
½ teaspoon sugar

Cut the corn off the cobs with a sharp knife, and scrape off as much juice as possible into the mixing bowl. Stir the cream into the corn, add the flour and seasonings and mix till smooth and well blended. Heat a griddle or large frying pan until very hot, grease it with a small piece of butter, and drop spoonfuls of the corn mixture onto it. Flatten them with a spatula and try to allow a few holes to develop in the little flat cakes. Cook until golden brown, turn and brown the other side, approximately 4 minutes each side.

    Serves 4–5.

PANCAKE BATTERS

Batter I (plain):
2 cups all-purpose flour
¼ teaspoon salt
2 eggs
1 cup milk
1 cup water

Sift the flour with the salt into a large bowl. Make a well in the center. Beat the eggs and pour them into the well. Mix the milk and water. Using a wire whisk, beat the eggs, incorporating the flour little by little around the edges, and pouring in the milk and water with the other hand. Do it carefully so that by the time the container of milk and water is empty all the flour has been drawn into the mixture. Continue to beat for two minutes, until perfectly smooth. Leave in a cool place for 1–2 hours, if possible, before using. The mixture should resemble fairly thick but unwhipped cream. If it is too thick, add a little more liquid before using. In any case, beat well for 1–2 minutes before cooking.

    This recipe makes a fairly large amount of batter. It can be cut in half or half of the prepared batter can be stored in the refrigerator until the following day. These pancakes make a good first course or main dish filled with any of the items on the pages that follow.

    Serves 6–8.

Batter II (wholewheat):
1 cup whole wheat flour
1 cup plain white flour
¼ teaspoon salt
2 eggs
1 cup milk
1 cup water

Make as for Batter I (plain). (The wholewheat flour absorbs more liquid, hence the extra milk and water.) This makes a more substantial pancake than the plain batter, suitable for a main course. Fill with spinach filling, *ratatouille*, or tomatoes in sour cream (see pages 55 and 82).

Serves 6–8.

Batter III (buckwheat):
1 cup buckwheat flour (obtainable from health food shops)
1 cup plain white flour
½ teaspoon salt
2 eggs
1 cup milk
1 cup water

Make as for Batter I (plain). (The buckwheat flour absorbs more liquid, so allow a little extra milk and water.) This makes a filling pancake, suitable for a main course. Fill with tomato and onion filling or mushrooms in sour cream.

Serves 6–8.

Batter IV (spinach):
½ pound raw spinach or
½ pound package frozen chopped spinach
batter I (see page 53)

Cook the spinach and drain as well as possible. Purée in a blender. Make the Batter I and stir in ½ cup spinach purée. Let stand for 2 hours before using. For a very smooth batter run through the blender again. This can be made in half quantities. It makes an unusual green pancake, excellent with tomato sauce, with a mushroom stuffing and served with a *sauce mornay*, or filled with mushrooms or tomatoes in sour cream.

Serves 6–8.

PANCAKE FILLINGS

Mushrooms in sour cream:
6 ounces mushrooms
2–3 tablespoons butter
½ cup sour cream
salt and black pepper

Slice the mushrooms and cook in the butter until soft. Add the sour cream, and season to taste.

Spinach filling:
1 pound spinach or 1 package frozen spinach
½ onion
2 tablespoons butter
1 teaspoon flour
½ cup sour cream
salt and black pepper

Cook the spinach in the usual way, drain it well and chop it. Chop the onion finely. Brown it in the butter; when soft, add the flour and blend. Stir in the cream and cook gently until smooth. Stir in the spinach, reheat, and season to taste. This makes an excellent filling for buckwheat or wholewheat pancakes.

Tomato and onion filling:
1 medium onion
¾ pound fresh tomatoes or
a 14-ounce can tomatoes
1 clove garlic
2 tablespoons butter
1 tablespoon olive oil
1 heaping teaspoon flour
salt and black pepper
sugar
ground celery seed
or substitute celery salt for plain salt
2 tablespoons chopped basil or marjoram

Chop the onion coarsely. If using fresh tomatoes, skin them and chop coarsely. Heat the butter and oil and cook the onion in a covered pan until the onions are soft, about 10 minutes, stirring now and then. Add the crushed garlic and cook another minute, then stir in the flour and cook for another minute before adding the tomatoes. Simmer until thick and soft, about 8 minutes. Season to taste. This makes 1 cup.

Tomatoes in sour cream:
¾ pound tomatoes
2 tablespoons butter
salt and black pepper
sugar
2 tablespoons chopped fresh basil, when available
½ cup sour cream

Skin the tomatoes and chop them coarsely. Melt the butter and cook the tomatoes until softened, about 5 minutes. Add salt and black pepper, a pinch of sugar, and fresh basil when available. Stir in the sour cream and cook gently until well mixed and blended, another 3—4 minutes. This filling is excellent with spinach pancakes.

To assemble pancakes: Spread 2—4 tablespoons of the filling in the center of each pancake and roll. Place rolled pancake in ovenproof dish. When all pancakes have been filled, reheat or broil until hot.

SPINACH PANCAKES

pancake batter IV (see page 54)
mushrooms in sour cream (see page 54)

Tomato sauce:
1 pound tomatoes
2 ounces butter
1 clove garlic
2 tablespoons chopped fresh basil, if available
salt and black pepper
sugar

Make the batter, and while it is standing make the mushroom filling. Then make the tomato sauce: skin and chop the tomatoes coarsely. Melt the butter and cook the tomatoes with the crushed garlic and basil for about 8 minutes, adding salt, black pepper and a pinch of sugar. Keep both fillings hot while you make the pancakes. Heat a griddle or large crêpe pan. When very hot, grease lightly with a small piece of butter. Pour half a ladleful of batter onto the center of the pan, and tilt to form a large thin crêpe. Make six in all, keeping them hot and assemble on a flat dish like a layer cake, in the following order: pancake, 1/3 of the mushroom filling, second pancake, 1/3 of the tomato sauce, third pancake, and so on, finishing with a layer of tomato sauce. Cut in quarters to serve.
Serves 4.

An excellent dish, very pretty and well worth the trouble.

[6]

Soufflés and Timbales

STEAMED BROCCOLI RING

½ pound broccoli
2 tablespoons butter
1½ tablespoons flour
½ cup thin cream
salt and black pepper
3 ounces grated Gruyère, Emmenthal
or Parmesan cheese
4 eggs

Cook the broccoli until just tender in lightly salted water. Drain well, reserving the liquid, and chop finely. Melt the butter, stir in the flour and cook for 3 minutes. Heat ½ cup of the reserved cooking water with the cream, and pour into the *roux*. Stir until smooth and cook gently for 4 minutes. Season quite highly with salt and black pepper, then stir in the grated cheese. When smooth, add the chopped broccoli and mix well. Remove from the fire and stir in the beaten egg yolks. Then beat the whites until stiff and fold in. Pour into a buttered ring mould. Set in a pan half full of water and steam for 40 minutes at 325 degrees. When set and lightly browned, invert onto a

flat dish. Serve with a garlic and yoghurt sauce (page 136) or tomato sauce (page 142).
Serves 4.

An alternate method is to cook the broccoli mixture in a soufflé dish for 20 minutes at 400 degrees.

ZUCCHINI SOUFFLE

1 cup cooked puréed zucchini (¾ pound uncooked)
4 tablespoons butter
3 tablespoons flour
½ cup cooking water
½ cup milk with a little cream added
2 tablespoons grated Parmesan cheese
salt and pepper
4 eggs, separated

To make the purée, slice the unpeeled zucchini in ½-inch slices and cook in just enough boiling water to cover, for 12 minutes. Drain, reserving the water, and mash with a fork or push through the coarse mesh of a vegetable mill. Dry out the purée for a few minutes in the cleaned pan, stirring over gentle heat. To make the soufflé mixture, melt the butter, stir in the flour and cook for 2 minutes. Heat the stock and milk together, blend into the *roux*, and simmer for 4 minutes. Stir in the cheese, and season with salt and pepper. Stir in the zucchini purée, mixing well. Remove from the heat and add beaten egg yolks. Whip the whites until they form stiff peaks and fold in. Pour into a buttered soufflé dish and bake for 25 minutes at 400 degrees.
Serves 4—5.

CARROT SOUFFLE

1 pound carrots
2½ cups chicken stock
salt and black pepper
1 teaspoon butter
1 teaspoon flour
2 eggs, separated

Slice the carrots and cook until tender in the stock. Drain, reserving the liquid. Purée in the blender with 6 tablespoons of the stock. Return the puréed mixture to the pan, and stir in a paste made by mixing the butter and flour. Drop in small pieces, stirring constantly until slightly thickened. Remove from the stove, and stir in the beaten egg yolks. Whip the egg whites until they are stiff, and fold into the soufflé mixture. Pour into a buttered dish and bake for 20 minutes at 350 degrees, or until slightly risen and set. Serve immediately.

Serves 3.

TIMBALE OF GREEN PEAS

1 pound shelled or frozen green peas
4 tablespoons soft bread crumbs
2 tablespoons milk
salt and black pepper
4 tablespoons softened butter
3 eggs, separated

Cook the peas in lightly salted boiling water for 5 minutes. While the peas are cooking, stir the bread crumbs into the milk to soak, squeezing them dry after a few minutes. Drain the peas and purée in the blender or push through medium mesh of the vegetable mill. Stir the bread crumbs into the purée, and season to taste. Beat in the softened butter, adding it by small pieces. Beat the egg yolks and stir into the mixture. Whip the egg whites and fold in. Pour into a buttered soufflé mold. Place the dish in a pan half-filled with water. Cover, bring the water to a boil and steam the timbale for 1 hour. To serve, invert on a hot plate and pour tomato sauce (page 142) over timbale.

Serves 3–4.

SPINACH SOUFFLE

1 pound spinach
or
½ pound frozen chopped spinach
4 tablespoons butter
1 cup milk or buttermilk

1 cup Philadelphia cream cheese
salt and pepper
4 eggs, separated

Clean the spinach thoroughly, and cook it for 5 minutes in a saucepan with only the water adhering to the leaves after washing. Turn into colander to drain. When cool enough to handle, squeeze the spinach in your hands until as much moisture as possible has been expressed. Chop it finely on a board. (If planning to serve a spinach sauce with the soufflé, cook an extra ½ pound spinach and reserve 1/3 of the chopped drained spinach for the sauce.) Melt the butter, blend with the flour and add the heated milk or buttermilk. Stir until a thick smooth sauce is obtained, then beat in the cream cheese, breaking it into small pieces as you add it. Beat until smooth and well mixed. Stir in the chopped spinach and season well. Cook slightly, then mix in the beaten egg yolks. When ready to cook, whip the egg whites until stiff, then fold into the mixture. Pour into a buttered soufflé dish and bake for 30 minutes at 350 degrees. Serve with a spinach sauce (page 145) or a mushroom and tomato sauce (page 140).
Serves 4–5.

TURNIP SOUFFLE

6 ounces cooked puréed turnip
(allow about ¾ pound raw turnips)
4 tablespoons butter
3 tablespoons flour
½ cup cooking water
½ cup milk
2 tablespoons finely chopped parsley
salt and black pepper
4 eggs, separated

Cook the turnips in water until tender, about 15 minutes. Reserve ½ cup of the water. Dry the purée by cooking it in a saucepan for several minutes. Melt the butter, and add the flour. Cook gently for 3 minutes, stirring constantly. Heat the milk and the reserved water together, and add to the butter and flour mixture. Stir until smooth, bring to a boil, and simmer for 5 minutes. Stir in the puréed turnips and chopped parsley and season to taste with salt and pepper. Remove from the heat, cool slightly, and add the beaten egg yolks. Whip the whites until stiff and fold gently into the mixture. Pour into a buttered soufflé dish and cook for 25 minutes at 400 degrees.

Serves 4–5.

This soufflé can also be made with parsnips or Jerusalem artichokes instead of turnips.

[7]

Individual Vegetable Dishes

TERRY'S EGGPLANT
---

2 large eggplants
1 Spanish onion
1 pound tomatoes
olive oil
salt and black pepper
sugar
¼ pound Mozzarella cheese, thinly sliced

Cut the eggplants in ½-inch slices, salt them, and leave to drain in a colander. Cut the onion in half, then cut each half in ¼-inch slices. Divide the slices into rings. Peel the tomatoes, discard the seeds and juice and cut them in strips like the onion. Rinse and dry the eggplants. Heat some olive oil in a large, heavy frying pan and fry the eggplant slices until brown on both sides. Place them on a dish and keep warm. Add more oil to the pan and cook the onion until it is soft, then add the tomatoes and cook the mixture a few minutes more. Season with salt, black pepper and a little sugar. Spoon the tomato and onion mixture over the eggplant slices and top with the sliced cheese. Bake at 350 degrees for 30 minutes.
    Serves 4.

FRIED EGGPLANT

2 medium-sized eggplants
flour
salt and black pepper
1—2 lemons, optional

Leave the eggplants unpeeled and cut across in very thin slices. Sprinkle them with salt and leave to drain for about 30 minutes, then rinse and pat dry. Coat the slices in seasoned flour by shaking them in a bag, then drop them one by one into a pan of hot oil. Do not try to cook too many at one time. Turn them over once so that they brown on both sides. In about 3—4 minutes they should be golden brown. Lift them out and drain. Keep them hot while you fry the next batch, but wait until the fat or oil has reheated before putting the second batch in. Serve with lemon quarters.
Serves 4.

STRING BEANS PROVENÇALE

1 pound string (green) beans
½ pound tomatoes
¼ pound tiny onions
1 clove garlic
2 tablespoons butter
2 tablespoons olive oil
salt and black pepper

Skin the tomatoes, cut them in half horizontally and remove the seeds with the point of a knife. Peel the onions. If they are really small, leave them whole; otherwise, cut them in half. Snap off the ends of the beans, leaving them whole. Mince or crush the garlic. Heat the butter and oil in a sauté pan with a lid. Put in the onions and cook gently until they are lightly colored, turning them around in the oil. Add the tomatoes, cut side downwards, and cook another 2—3 minutes. Add the beans, garlic, salt and black pepper, cover the pan and cook gently for 40 minutes, stirring now and then. Test the beans to make sure they are just tender before serving. This is also good cold.
Serves 6.

BRAISED ENDIVE

1½ pounds endive
3 tablespoons butter
2 tablespoons lemon juice
1–2 tablespoons water
salt and black pepper

Bring a large pan of water to a boil, throw in the endive, cook for 5 minutes and drain. Rub a shallow sauté pan with some of the butter, put in the endive in one layer, and dot with the remaining butter. Squeeze over about 2 tablespoons lemon juice, and sprinkle with salt and black pepper. Add 1 tablespoon water, cover and cook gently for 45 minutes, turning the endive over from time to time. If the liquid shows signs of boiling away, add another tablespoon of water.

Serves 4.

BRAISED CELERY HEARTS

3 heads celery
4 tablespoons butter
¾ cup stock:
beef, chicken, game, veal or vegetable
about 1 tablespoon lemon juice
salt and black pepper

Bring a large pan of water to a boil. Remove the outside stalks of the celery, trim the stumps, and cut the inner stalks down to make a neat heart. Cut each heart in half and throw into the boiling water. Cook for 5 minutes, then drain. Rub a heavy pan with some of the butter and lay the celery hearts in it in one layer. Dot with the remaining butter. Pour in the stock and add salt, black pepper and the lemon juice. Cover with the lid and cook very gently on top of the stove for 40–60 minutes, depending on the size and age of the celery. Turn them over every half hour, and add a little more stock if necessary. After 1½ hours test with a skewer to see if they are soft. Remove them to a clean dish and pour the juice over them, or thicken it slightly by stirring in 1 teaspoon flour rubbed into 1 teaspoon butter. Stir until smooth and slightly thickened, taste for seasoning, and pour over the celery.

Serves 6.

BRAISED FENNEL

3 heads fennel
4 tablespoons butter
¾ cup stock:
beef, chicken, game or vegetable
1 tablespoon lemon juice
salt and black pepper
1 teaspoon butter
1 teaspoon flour

Trim the fennel, cutting off any discolored leaves and scrubbing well under running water. Cut each root in half and lay them in one layer in a sauté pan. Cut the butter in small pieces and scatter over them. Pour over the stock and add the lemon juice, salt and black pepper. Cover with the lid and cook very gently on top of the stove for 1½−2 hours, turning from time to time, and adding more stock if necessary. When they are soft (test by piercing with a fork), transfer them to a shallow dish and thicken the juice slightly by stirring in the butter and flour which you have mixed to a paste. Stir till smooth and pour over the fennel.
    Serves 4−6.

VIENNESE-STYLE RED CABBAGE

1 large red cabbage
1 Spanish onion
6 tablespoons beef drippings
2 tablespoons sugar
1 large cooking apple
3 tablespoons red wine vinegar
salt and black pepper
1 cup beef stock
1 tablespoon flour
¼ cup sour cream

Cut the cabbage in quarters, discard the outer leaves and the central core, then shred each quarter finely. Chop the onion. Melt the fat in a deep heavy casserole and cook the onion until it starts to soften and color. Add the sugar and stir until golden. Put in the cabbage and mix well. Chop the unpeeled apple and add to the cabbage. Add the vinegar and season with salt and black pepper. Stir well, cover and cook for 15 minutes over a low flame. Heat the stock and pour into the casserole. Cook for 2 hours on top of the stove or in the oven at 310 degrees. When done, mix the flour and cream to a paste and add to the cabbage by degrees, stirring all the time, on top of the stove. Cook over a low flame for 3—4 minutes to cook the flour and thicken the sauce. Taste, and add more sugar or vinegar if necessary—the sweet and sour elements should be nicely balanced—or more salt and black pepper.

 Serves 8.

This dish is improved by being made a day in advance and reheated in a covered casserole in a moderate oven (350 degrees) for 1 hour. Excellent with game, boiled ham, bacon, and sausages of all sorts.

ZUCCHINI IN CHEESE SOUFFLE SAUCE

2 large zucchini
or
4 smaller ones

Cheese soufflé sauce:
4 tablespoons butter
3 tablespoons flour
1 cup milk
3 ounces grated Gruyère cheese
2 eggs, separated

Poach the whole zucchinis in boiling salted water for 10 minutes, then drain. Cut a thin sliver off two opposite sides of the zucchini to flatten, then cut lengthwise into slices about 1/3 inch thick. (If using small zucchinis, cut in half, after removing a very thin sliver to flatten the base.) Lay each slice on a greased baking sheet. Make the sauce: melt the butter, stir in the flour, and cook for 3 minutes, stirring continuously. Add the heated milk, and stir till smooth. Simmer for 5 minutes, stirring now and then, then beat in the grated cheese. Stir over gentle heat till melted and smooth. Season well with salt and black pepper. Remove from the heat and beat in the beaten egg yolks. Whip the whites until stiff, then fold into the sauce. Using two teaspoons, cover each of the zucchini slices with the sauce, heaping it up thickly. Place the baking sheet in the oven preheated to 400 degrees, and cook for 15 minutes, when the sauce should be puffed up and golden brown. Serve immediately.

Serves 4.

CREAMED LEEKS

2 pounds leeks
3 tablespoons butter
½ tablespoon flour
salt and black pepper
pinch grated nutmeg
½ cup cream

Wash and trim the leeks, and cut in 1-inch slices. Bring ½ inch lightly salted water to a boil in a heavy pan and put in the leeks. Cover the pan and cook for 10 minutes, shaking the pan from side to side occasionally. Drain the water, reserving it for later use. Shake the leeks about over gentle heat for a few minutes to dry them out, then turn onto a flat surface and chop. You should have about 2½ cups chopped leeks. Melt the butter in the cleaned pan, put in the leeks and reheat. Add the flour, stir to blend for 1 minute, then pour in ½ cup of the reserved cooking water (if there is less than ½ cup, add water) reheated in a small pan with the cream. Stir till well mixed and blended. Season well with salt and black pepper, and a little freshly grated nutmeg. Simmer for a few minutes, then pour into a serving dish and surround with croutons.

Serves 6.

SPINACH PUREE

2 pounds raw spinach
or
1½ pounds frozen spinach
3 tablespoons butter
1 small onion
1 clove garlic (optional)
1 teaspoon flour
½ pint thin cream
salt and black pepper

Cook the washed spinach very gently in the water clinging to its leaves, or, if frozen spinach is used, follow package directions. Stir now and then. When it releases its moisture turn up the heat slightly and add salt. When tender, drain very well and chop roughly with a knife. Melt the butter in the cleaned pan, chop the onion very finely and stew gently in the butter until soft. Add the minced or crushed garlic halfway through; do not allow to burn. Stir in the flour, blend with the heated cream, and season well with salt and black pepper. When smooth and blended, stir in the chopped spinach. Stir well, pour into the blender to make a purée. Return briefly to the pan to reheat and adjust seasoning. If serving alone, surround with garlic croutons.

Serves 4.

FRENCH BEANS WITH BACON

1 pound very small string beans
4 ounces bacon
1 teaspoon butter
salt and black pepper
1 small onion

Snap off the ends of the beans but leave them whole. Bring a pan of lightly salted water to boil, throw in the beans, and cook until just tender, about 8 minutes. Drain. Chop the bacon, melt the butter in a frying pan and fry the bacon slowly until crisp. Add the beans to the pan and stir around until well mixed and hot. Add salt and black pepper to taste. Pile on a flat serving dish and scatter the very finely chopped raw onion over the top.

Serves 6.

DRIED BEANS PROVENCALE

2 cups dried haricot beans
½ pound tomatoes
2 tablespoons olive oil
1 clove garlic
salt and black pepper
3 tablespoons finely chopped parsley

Soak the beans for 2—3 hours, then cover with cold water and bring to a boil. Simmer gently till soft, about 1—2 hours, adding salt towards the end. Heat the oil and cook the skinned and chopped tomatoes with the minced garlic for about 5 minutes, till softened. Add the beans and cook another 5 minutes, till well mixed and heated. Stir in the parsley and add salt and black pepper to taste.

Serves 4.

HOME BAKED BEANS

1½ cups dried haricot beans
1 tablespoon olive oil
1 medium onion
2 ounces bacon
2 cloves garlic
salt and black pepper
2—3 tablespoons chopped parsley

Soak the beans for about 3 hours, then drain. Chop the onion and cook in the oil until it starts to soften. Dice the bacon and add to the onion. Mince the garlic finely and add to the bacon. Pour in the drained beans, barely cover with cold water, and add salt and black pepper. Cover the casserole and bake at 275 degrees for 2 hours or until the beans are tender, stir once or twice adding water if necessary. Drain off any excess liquid and stir in 2—3 tablespoons chopped parsley before serving.

Serves 4—6.

BEETS WITH DILL

1½ pounds cooked beets
2 tablespoons butter
½ cup cream
2 tablespoons chopped fresh dill
salt and black pepper

Cut the beets in quarters if small, or in chunks or thick slices if larger. Melt the butter in a sauté pan and stir the beets in it until coated all over with the butter, and quite hot. Pour in the cream and add plenty of salt and black pepper. Stir until well mixed and hot. Sprinkle on the chopped dill and serve.

Serves 4—6.

BEETS IN SOUR CREAM

1½ pounds small beets, cooked
2 tablespoons butter
½ cup sour cream, room temperature
salt and black pepper

Cut the beets in thick slices and toss in butter in a sauté pan until coated all over. Pour in the sour cream and season well with salt and black pepper. Put on the lid and leave over a very gentle heat for about 8 minutes to heat through. Stir occasionally.

Serves 4—6.

CARROT PUREE

1 pound carrots
2 tablespoons butter
salt and black pepper

Slice the carrots and cover with cold water. Add salt, bring to a boil, and simmer about 20 minutes till soft. Drain and return to the pan to dry out, stirring for 2 minutes over a gentle heat. Push the carrots through the medium mesh of a vegetable mill and return the purée to the pan, stir over low heat to dry out as much moisture as possible, then beat in the butter. Season with salt and black pepper and serve.

Serves 4.

CAULIFLOWER POLONAISE

1 medium cauliflower
4 tablespoons butter
4 tablespoons bread crumbs
lemon juice
1 hard-boiled egg
2 tablespoons chopped parsley
salt and black pepper

Cook the cauliflower until just tender in boiling salted water. Drain upside down in a colander. Place on a round serving dish and keep hot. Melt the butter, and when it is very hot put in the bread crumbs and stir around until all are well browned, being careful not to let them burn. Add the chopped egg and the parsley, stir over a gentle heat until all are well mixed and hot, adding a little lemon juice and salt and black pepper to taste. Pour over the whole cauliflower and serve.

Serves 4.

CAULIFLOWER COOKED IN STOCK

1 cauliflower
3 tablespoons butter
about 1 cup chicken stock
salt and black pepper

Divide cauliflower into sprigs and chop. Melt 2 tablespoons butter in a heavy pan, put in the cauliflower and stir over low heat for 4–5 minutes. Pour on enough boiling stock to cover half the cauliflower, add salt and cover the pan. Simmer until just tender, and the liquid is almost evaporated. If there is still much left, remove the cauliflower with a slotted spoon and keep warm while you boil up the stock to reduce to a few spoonfuls. Add the remaining butter and a little black pepper and pour over the cauliflower.

Serves 4–5.

GRATIN OF ENDIVE

1½ pounds endive
3 tablespoons butter
1 teaspoon lemon juice
2 eggs
½ cup thick cream
salt and black pepper
nutmeg
1 ounce grated Gruyère cheese

Cut the endive in 1-inch slices. Cook gently in the butter and lemon juice in a covered sauté pan for 10 minutes, stirring once or twice. Drain the endive in a colander while you beat the eggs with the cream, adding salt, black pepper, nutmeg to taste, and the cheese. (This amount of cheese will give only a very slight flavor; if you want a stronger cheese taste, double the quantity.) Mix the drained endive with the egg and cream mixture and pour into a buttered gratin dish. Cook for 15 minutes at 400 degrees.

Serves 4.

GRATIN OF ZUCCHINI

1½ pounds zucchini
2 eggs
½ cup thick cream
salt and black pepper
nutmeg
2 ounces grated Gruyère cheese

Cut the zucchini in ½-inch slices, cook them for 12 minutes in boiling salted water and drain. Press them in a colander to get rid of as much moisture as possible. Turn them into a greased shallow ovenproof dish. Beat the eggs with the cream, season with salt and pepper, add nutmeg to taste, and the cheese. Pour mixture over the zucchini. Cook at 400 degrees for 15 minutes until slightly risen and browned.

Serves 4–5.

STEWED ZUCCHINI WITH TOMATOES

1 pound zucchini
3 tablespoons butter
½ pound tomatoes
salt and black pepper
1–2 tablespoons chopped basil, chervil or parsley

Cut the unpeeled zucchini in ½-inch slices, throw into boiling salted water and cook for 8 minutes. Drain in a colander. Melt the butter, add the peeled and roughly chopped tomatoes and simmer for 4–5 minutes. Add the zucchini and simmer for another 4–5 minutes. Add salt and black pepper to taste, sprinkle with chopped herbs and serve.

Serves 4–6.

POACHED ZUCCHINI WITH HERBS

1 pound zucchini
3 tablespoons butter
2 tablespoons chopped dill or chervil

Cut the unpeeled zucchini in ¾-inch slices, throw them in a pan of boiling salted water and cook for 10 minutes. Drain in a colander. Melt the butter in a covered sauté pan and toss the zucchini in it. Add the chopped herbs, cover and stew gently for 4 minutes.
Serves 4.

CORN PUDDING

4 ears corn
or
2 cups frozen or canned corn
3 eggs
2 cups half and half
2 tablespoons butter
1 teaspoon salt
1 teaspoon sugar
black pepper

Scrape the corn off the cobs, being careful not to waste any of the juice. Put the corn in a bowl and add the beaten eggs, the milk, the melted butter, and the salt, sugar and black pepper. Have a buttered soufflé dish ready and pour the corn into it. Bake at 350 degrees for 45 minutes.
Serves 6.

BAKED CORN

6 ears corn
4 tablespoons butter
salt and black pepper

Cut the corn kernels off the cobs, using a sharp knife and cutting downwards onto a flat surface. Then scrape the cobs well with the edge of the knife to get as much as possible of the milk (this is best done into a bowl).

Put the corn and the juice into a buttered baking dish, add the butter cut in small pieces, and plenty of salt and black pepper. Cook for 45 minutes at 350 degrees.

Serves 3–4.

CUCUMBERS STEWED IN CREAM

2 cucumbers
4 tablespoons butter
4 tablespoons cream
salt and black pepper

Peel the cucumbers and cut them in 1-inch chunks. Slice lengthwise, sprinkle with salt, and allow to drain for 30 minutes. Pat dry. Melt the butter in a sauté pan, put in the cucumber, and cover the pan. Cook gently for 10 minutes, shaking the pan occasionally. Add the cream, reheat, season and serve.

Serves 4–6.

A light moist dish that goes well with other vegetable dishes, as well as with veal or chicken.

CELERIAC PUREE

1 celeriac, about 1 pound
½ pound potatoes
4 tablespoons butter
4 tablespoons cream
salt and black pepper
1 tablespoon finely chopped parsley

Peel the celeriac and cut in chunks. Cover with cold water, add a little salt, and boil until tender when pierced with a fork, 25–30 minutes. Peel the potatoes and boil until tender. Drain both vegetables and dry out slightly over gentle heat. Force through the medium mesh of a vegetable mill. Return to the cleaned pan and beat the purée over a low flame. Add the butter and the cream, beating all the time. Season well with salt and black pepper. Pour into a serving dish and sprinkle with finely chopped parsley.

Serves 4.

CHINESE CABBAGE

1 Chinese cabbage
about 1 cup chicken stock
salt and black pepper
lemon juice

Cut the cabbage in slices. Put ½-inch chicken stock in the bottom of a heavy saucepan, bring to a boil and pile in the cabbage. Cook until tender, about 8–10 minutes, stirring often. There should be very little stock left. Serve in its own juice, adding salt, black pepper and a small amount of lemon juice to taste.
Serves 4.

MUSHROOMS IN SOUR CREAM

1 pound mushrooms
4 tablespoons butter
1 cup sour cream
salt and black pepper
lemon juice

Wipe the mushrooms, trim the stalks and slice. Heat the butter in a sauté pan and add the mushrooms. Stir until coated with butter and leave to stew gently until they have softened, about 8 minutes, stirring occasionally. Pour in the cream and stir to mix well. Simmer gently for 3–4 minutes, season with salt and black pepper, and add a little lemon juice to taste. Serve immediately.
Serves 4.

STEWED MUSHROOMS

1 pound mushrooms
6–8 tablespoons sunflower-seed oil
or
nut oil
2 large cloves garlic
salt and black pepper
2 tablespoons chopped parsley
lemon juice

Slice the mushrooms. Heat the oil in a small frying pan and cook the sliced mushrooms in it, turning them over now and then, until all are softened. Add more oil as necessary. Season with salt and black pepper, squeeze over lemon juice to taste, and sprinkle with chopped parsley.

Serves 3–4.

BRAISED ONIONS

1 pound Spanish onions
4 tablespoons beef dripping
or
cooking oil
1 cup meat or poultry stock
1 teaspoon butter
1 teaspoon flour
2 tablespoons cream
salt and black pepper

Slice the onions and cook them gently in the melted fat for about 8 minutes. Heat the stock and add to the onions. Simmer uncovered for 30 minutes, stirring occasionally. Work the butter and flour into a paste in a cup and add by degrees to thicken the sauce. Simmer till smooth, stirring constantly. Add the cream, season well and serve. Good with hard-boiled eggs.

Serves 4.

TURNIPS WITH MUSTARD

1½ pounds small turnips
2 tablespoons butter
1 tablespoon Dijon mustard
salt and black pepper
2 tablespoons freshly chopped parsley

Cut the turnips in ¾-inch slices, cover with cold water, add a little salt and bring to a boil. Cook until tender, about 12–15 minutes if they are really young, and drain well. Melt the butter in the cleaned and dried pan and turn the slices around in it until they are coated all over, but do not fry. Stir in the mustard, season with salt and black pepper and serve in a shallow dish sprinkled with parsley.

Serves 4–6.

TOMATOES WITH MOZZARELLA

4 large tomatoes or 6 medium ones
salt and black pepper
6–8 ounces Mozzarella cheese

Cut the unpeeled tomatoes in ½-inch slices. Arrange them on a large flat ovenproof dish or divide them between as many individual dishes as you have guests. Sprinkle the tomato slices with salt and black pepper. Cut the cheese in ¼-inch slices and lay over the tomatoes. Bake at 400 degrees about 15 minutes, or until the cheese has melted and become golden brown.

Serves 4–6 as a first course, 2 as a main dish.

BAKED TOMATOES

1½ pounds tomatoes
2 tablespoons butter
salt and black pepper
½ cup sour cream

Cut 1 pound tomatoes in half horizontally. Butter a shallow ovenproof dish and arrange the tomatoes in it. Dot with the butter and sprinkle with salt and black pepper. Bake at 350 degrees for 20 minutes. Meanwhile peel the remaining tomatoes and put in the blender with the sour cream. Season with salt and black pepper and heat till boiling in a small pan. When the tomatoes are cooked, pour the sauce over them and serve.

Serves 4–6.

[8]

Combined Vegetable Dishes

ZUCCHINI AND TOMATO CASSEROLE

¾ pound zucchini
1 pound tomatoes
4 large slices stale white bread, crusts removed
4 tablespoons melted butter
¼ pound cheese:
mozzarella, Gruyère or cheddar, sliced thin
1 heaping tablespoon chopped fresh basil, when available
salt and black pepper

Slice the unpeeled zucchini very thin and sprinkle them with salt. Leave for about 30 minutes, then rinse and pat dry. Skin the tomatoes and slice thin. Cut the bread in cubes and pour the melted butter over them. Butter a soufflé dish and put half the zucchini slices in one layer in the bottom. Season lightly, then lay half the tomatoes over them. Scatter half the basil over the tomatoes, and a sprinkling of sugar. Lay half the cheese slices over the tomatoes, then cover with half the buttered bread cubes. Repeat the layers, sprinkling with salt and black pepper, finishing with the remaining bread. Bake for about 1 hour at 375 degrees.

Serves 4.

EASY VEGETABLE STEW

1 eggplant, about ½ pound
½ pound zucchini
½ pound string beans
1 pound tomatoes
1 onion
2 potatoes
1 green pepper
1 cup olive oil
1 cup hot water
salt and black pepper
2 tablespoons parsley

Cut the unpeeled eggplant into quarters and slice thin. Slice the zucchini. Chop the beans into 1-inch pieces. Peel the tomatoes and cut into slices. Slice the onion and the peeled potatoes. Put all the vegetables into a casserole and pour over the oil and hot water. Throw in the chopped parsley, salt and black pepper. Bring to the boiling point on the stove, then cover the dish and bake at 350 degrees for 1½ hours. (This may also be cooked for the same amount of time over low heat on top of the stove.) Stir occasionally.
    Serves 4–6.

This simply made dish is good either hot or cold, or it can be made in double quantities and eaten hot the first day, then cold the following day.

MIXED VEGETABLE MOLD

¾ pound young parsnips
¾ pound young carrots
¾ pound young turnips
salt and pepper
¼ cup butter

Herb sauce:
½ cup butter
4 tablespoons chopped mixed herbs:
parsley, chervil, tarragon, dill
lemon juice

Grate each vegetable coarsely, keeping in separate piles. Butter a charlotte mold or other baking dish very thoroughly. Make a layer of the grated parsnips in the bottom of the dish and sprinkle with salt and black pepper. Cover with a layer of carrots, more salt and pepper to taste, then with a layer of turnips. Pour ¼ cup melted butter over the mixture. Cover with foil and bake at 350 degrees for 1 hour, then turn out onto a plate. To make the sauce, heat the remaining butter with the chopped herbs and season with lemon juice to taste. Pour over the mold and serve immediately.

Serves 6.

MIXED VEGETABLE CASSEROLE

6 small onions
6 new potatoes
4 small leeks
4 small zucchini
4 stalks celery
6 small carrots
½ pound tomatoes
1 small cauliflower
4½ tablespoons butter
2½ cups chicken or vegetable stock
1 teaspoon flour

Leave the onions and potatoes whole. Cut the leeks, zucchini and celery in 1-inch slices. Cut the carrots in half. Peel and quarter the tomatoes. Divide the cauliflower into sprigs. Melt 4 tablespoons butter and stew the onions gently in it, adding the leeks, zucchini, celery and tomatoes after a few minutes. Heat the stock and add it. Put in the potatoes and cauliflower, bring to the boil and simmer until all the vegetables are tender, about 1 hour. Mix the remaining butter and flour to a paste in a cup, and add by degrees to thicken the sauce. Simmer for 3 minutes to cook the flour, stir in the parsley and serve.

Serves 6.

RATATOUILLE

1 Spanish onion
2 large red peppers
2 large green peppers
1 pound zucchini
1 pound tomatoes
3–4 cloves garlic
approximately ½ cup sunflower-seed oil
salt and black pepper

Chop the onions, cut the peppers in strips, slice the zucchini and skin and chop the tomatoes. Mince the garlic. Heat some oil in a large pan, put in the chopped onions and cook until slightly softened, about 10 minutes. Add the peppers and cook for another 10 minutes; add the zucchini and cook another 10 minutes, then mix in the tomatoes and minced garlic, adding more oil as required to prevent sticking. Cook until the mixture is softened and well mixed, a further 10–15 minutes. Season well with salt and black pepper, and serve hot, warm or cold. Like many dishes this is best made a day in advance to allow the flavors to develop, and reheated.
     Serves 4–6.

This is the author's version of ratatouille. By omitting the eggplant and substituting sunflower-seed oil for olive oil, it makes a much lighter dish than the traditional French ratatouille.

ZUCCHINI, CARROTS AND TOMATOES

1 pound zucchini
¼ pound new carrots
½ pound tomatoes
olive oil
salt and black pepper

Slice the carrots and parboil for 5 minutes. Drain. Cut the unpeeled zucchini into slices about ½-inch thick. Skin the tomatoes and slice. Cover the bottom of a sauté pan with olive oil. Add the zucchini when the oil is sizzling and cook gently for 10 minutes with the lid on, stirring frequently. Add the carrots and cook for another 10 minutes. Add the tomatoes and cook 15 minutes more, until the mixture is soft and slightly mushy. Season with salt and pepper.

Serves 4.

This makes a delicious vegetable dish on its own, faintly like a ratatouille, and is excellent used as a filling for pancakes.

LEEKS AND CARROTS

2 pounds leeks
1 pound carrots
3½ tablespoons butter
salt and black pepper
2 tablespoons chopped parsley

Cut the leeks in 1-inch slices, cook for 10 minutes in a covered pan in ½-inch lightly salted water. Drain well. Cut the carrots in ½-inch slices, cook until tender in boiling salted water and drain. Melt the butter in a heavy pan, put in the carrots and leeks and mix well. Add plenty of salt and black pepper; stew gently until vegetables are well heated and softened.

Serves 4–6.

GREEN PEAS WITH CUCUMBER

3 pounds fresh peas in the pod
or
1 package frozen *petits pois*
1 cucumber
4 tablespoons butter
sprig of mint
1 teaspoon sugar
salt and black pepper

Dice the cucumber coarsely. Bring ½ inch lightly salted water to a boil in a heavy pan and throw in the cucumber and the shelled peas. Add the butter, mint, sugar, salt and black pepper. Cook gently in the covered pan, shaking from time to time, until the peas are tender. Do not drain but serve in their cooking liquor. If using frozen peas, cook the cucumber alone in the butter for 5–8 minutes, then add the peas and 2 tablespoons only water. Cook another 4–5 minutes, until the peas and cucumber are cooked.

Serves 4.

Excellent with salmon, trout, or with veal.

PEPERONATA

2 pounds peppers,
mixed red, green and yellow if possible
1 Spanish onion
1 pound tomatoes
about ½ cup olive oil
or
sunflower seed oil
2 cloves garlic (optional)
salt and black pepper

Remove the stalks and seeds from the peppers. Cut the flesh in strips. Chop the onion; skin and chop the tomatoes. Heat the oil in a sauté pan and add the onion. Cook gently for 5 minutes, then add the peppers. Cover and stew slowly for 15 minutes, then add the tomatoes and the minced garlic, stir well, and cook for another 10–15 minutes. Season well with salt and black pepper. Serve hot, warm or cold.
Serves 4–6.

This makes an excellent filling for pancakes.

SUCCOTASH

about 1 cup fresh corn
about 1 cup lima beans
3 tablespoons butter
salt and black pepper

It is difficult to give exact quantities for this dish, as much depends on the size and age of the vegetables, but the quantities should be roughly equal. Cook the corn in very little boiling salted water until just tender and drain. Cook the beans in the same way; if using broad beans, the outer skins should be removed before or after cooking. When both vegetables are well drained, mix and stir over a gentle heat with the butter and plenty of salt and black pepper.
Serves 4.

COLD STUFFED TOMATOES

6 large tomatoes

Cucumber and cheese filling:
½ pound cottage or cream cheese
2 tablespoons lemon juice
2 tablespoons olive oil
or
sunflower-seed oil
salt and pepper
½ cucumber, diced (1 cup)
4 tablespoons chopped chives

Mix together lightly the ingredients for the filling. Skin the tomatoes by covering with boiling water for exactly 1 minute, then plunging into cold water. Do not leave a moment longer as they must stay firm. Cut a slice off the tops and remove the insides carefully with a small sharp-edged teaspoon. Sprinkle the insides with salt and leave to drain upside down for 20 minutes. Shake dry, sprinkle a pinch of sugar into each tomato, and divide the filling among them. Chill again or serve immediately.

Serves 6 as a first course.

BRAISED ROOT VEGETABLES

½ pound carrots
½ pound parsnips
½ pound turnips
3 tablespoons beef dripping or butter
1¼ cups beef stock
salt and black pepper
2 tablespoons chopped parsley

Cut the vegetables in thin slices. Melt the fat in a heavy sauté pan and add the vegetables. Stir until coated with fat, and cook gently for 5 minutes, stirring now and then. Heat the stock and pour on, cover the pan and simmer for 20–30 minutes, until vegetables are soft. Stir occasionally. Season well with salt and black pepper and serve sprinkled with chopped parsley.

Serves 4–5.

STUFFED EGGPLANT

3 eggplants
about 6 tablespoons olive oil
about 6 tablespoons butter
1½ pounds tomatoes
1 Spanish onion
2 cloves garlic
2 tablespoons dry bread crumbs
salt and black pepper
2 tablespoons chopped parsley

Cut the unpeeled eggplants in half lengthwise. Run a small knife around the edge between the skin and the flesh, without puncturing the skin. Sprinkle the cut surface with salt and turn upside down to drain for 30 minutes. Heat about 2 tablespoons each of oil and butter in a big frying pan. Rinse and dry the eggplants and cook them in the oil and butter, allowing about 6–8 minutes on each side. Drain again. When cool enough to handle remove the flesh from the skins, taking care to leave the skins intact. Chop the flesh. Peel the tomatoes, discard the juice and seeds and chop the flesh. Chop the onion and mince or crush 1 clove garlic. Heat about 1 tablespoon each of oil and butter in the same pan and cook the chopped onion in it until soft. Add the eggplant, tomatoes and garlic. Cook all together for 15 minutes, stirring often and seasoning well with salt and black pepper. Fill the skins with the mixture. Toss the bread crumbs in more hot butter with a peeled clove of garlic; when lightly browned, discard the garlic and mix in the parsley. Stir till nicely mixed, scatter over the top of the eggplants, and cook in a moderate oven (350 degrees) for 30 minutes.

Serves 6 as an accompaniment to a main course, or 3 as a separate course.

STUFFED CABBAGE

1 green cabbage

Stuffing:
1 pound mixed greens: lettuce, spinach,
watercress, dandelion, endive, sorrel
½ cup uncooked rice
1 onion

¼ pound sliced ham
¼ pound mushrooms
salt and black pepper
chicken stock

Have as varied and tasty a mixture of greens as you can. After washing, throw them into a large pan of boiling water and cook for 4 minutes. Drain, reserving the water in the pan, and cool. When cool enough to handle, squeeze between the hands to press out as much moisture as possible. Turn onto a board and chop. Choose 5 or 6 large perfect cabbage leaves and blanch in the same water for 4 minutes. Drain. To make the stuffing, wash the rice, drain and put it in a large bowl. Slice or chop the onion and mix with the rice. Chop the ham and the mushrooms, and add to the stuffing. Stir in the chopped greens and add 2 teaspoons salt and plenty of black pepper. Lay a clean piece of muslin in a baking dish and arrange 4–5 of the cabbage leaves in it to form a casing. Spoon the stuffing in carefully and cover with another leaf. Tie the muslin around it loosely, remembering that the rice will swell. Bring a large pan of chicken stock (enough to cover the cabbage) to a boil and pour over the mixture. Cover with the lid and simmer for 1 hour. Lift out and drain for a minute, then untie the muslin and turn the cabbage out carefully onto a serving dish. Serve with a tomato sauce.

Serves 4.

STUFFED CABBAGE LEAVES

2 ounces rice
1 small onion
1 ounce fat
salt and black pepper
1 pound raw minced pork
1 green cabbage
3 cups beef or chicken stock
1 tablespoon butter
1 tablespoon flour
1 egg yolk
¼ cup sour cream

Boil the rice until barely tender. Drain. Chop the onion finely and brown it in the fat in a frying pan. Add the pork and cook lightly, stirring often, till browned. Add the drained rice and mix well. Season with salt and black pepper and leave to cool. Separate the cabbage leaves, discarding the outermost ones. Cut out the thickest part of the stalk in a V-shape, and throw them, a few at a time, into a large pan of boiling water. Let them cook for 4 minutes, then lift them out and drain, while you cook the others. When cool, wrap each one around a mound of the stuffing, making a little enclosed roll. Cut up the unused leaves in strips and lay at the bottom of a casserole. Lay the stuffed leaves on top of this bed. Heat the stock and pour over enough almost to cover them. Cover with a lid and cook in a moderate oven (350 degrees) for 45 minutes. Drain off the stock, reserving 1 cup for the sauce. Melt the butter, stir in the flour and add stock to make a thin sauce. Stir until cooked, adding salt and black pepper to taste. Beat the egg yolk with the sour cream, stir in a little of the boiling stock, and return the sauce to the pan. Stir until smooth, without allowing it to boil. Arrange the cabbage leaves in a dish. Pour the sauce over the cabbage or pass separately.

Serves 6.

COLD STUFFED LEAVES OF CHINESE CABBAGE

1 Chinese cabbage
½ cup uncooked rice
2 ounces chopped almonds
or whole pine kernels
½ pound tomatoes, skinned and diced
1 bunch scallions or 1 medium onion, chopped
½ cup chopped parsley
1½ teaspoons sea salt
black pepper
about 1 cup chicken stock
lemon juice

Choose about 12 perfect leaves of the Chinese cabbage and blanch them by throwing for 1 minute into a pan of boiling water. Drain. To make the stuffing wash and drain the rice, and put it in a large bowl. Add the chopped almonds, the sliced scallions or chopped onion, the skinned and chopped tomatoes and the chopped parsley. Add the salt and plenty of black pepper and mix well. Spread each cabbage leaf carefully on a board, being careful not to tear them as they are very fragile, and lay about 1½ tablespoons stuffing on each one. Roll them up. Slice the remaining cabbage and put in the bottom of a broad saucepan to make a bed for the stuffed leaves. Lay the wrapped leaves on top and pour over enough stock to half cover them. Bring to a boil and simmer for 30 minutes. Lift out the stuffed leaves and lay them on a flat dish. Sprinkle generously with lemon juice and leave to cool. Serve cold, with more lemon.

Serves 3–4.

When Chinese cabbage is not available, substitute romaine.

STUFFED GREEN PEPPERS

1 medium onion
2–3 tablespoons nut oil
1 clove garlic
2 tablespoons pine kernels
½ cup rice
2½ cups chicken stock
1 tablespoon raisins
salt and black pepper
pinch of mace or grated nutmeg
pinch of cinnamon
2 tablespoons chopped parsley
2 tablespoons butter
6 green peppers

To make the filling, chop the onion and cook in oil in a frying pan until slightly colored. Add the minced or crushed garlic and the pine kernels, and cook another 2–3 minutes. Add the washed rice and stir around until coated with oil. Pour on 1¼ cups heated stock, add the raisins, salt, pepper and spices and simmer until the rice is almost tender, about 15 minutes, stirring now and then. Leave to cool. To prepare the peppers cut a thin slice off the top and remove the interior membrane and all the seeds with a small sharp knife. Rinse with water to remove any remaining seeds. Spoon in the stuffing when it has cooled, and stand the peppers upright in a deep ovenproof dish with a lid. Heat the remaining stock with the butter and pour on. Cover with the lid of a double layer of foil and cook in a moderate oven (350 degrees) for 45 minutes. Serve hot or cold with a bowl of yoghurt or garlic sauce with yoghurt.

Serves 6.

This filling can be used in the same way for stuffing other vegetables, or made in larger quantities and served as a pilaf, in which case increase the quantity of stock in proportion to the rice by half, and cook the rice for an extra 10 minutes.

COLD STUFFED MUSHROOMS

---

6 large flat mushrooms
olive oil

Eggplant salad filling:
2 medium-sized eggplants
½ Spanish onion
½ pound tomatoes
salt and pepper
3 tablespoons olive oil
1 tablespoon lemon juice or white wine vinegar
2 tablespoons finely chopped parsley

Lay the mushrooms on a baking sheet with the gills uppermost, and brush them lightly with olive oil. Cook in the oven at 350 degrees until soft, about 20 minutes. Remove from the oven and leave to cool. Make the eggplant filling, following instructions for eggplant salad on page 112. When the mushrooms are cool, spoon the filling onto them, and sprinkle with finely chopped parsley.

Serves 6 as a first course.

[9]

Potatoes and Grains

BOXTY

½ pound mashed potatoes
½ pound raw potatoes
1 small onion, put through a garlic press
1 large egg
2 tablespoons flour
4 tablespoons melted butter
1 teaspoon sea salt
½ teaspoon black pepper

Peel and grate the raw potatoes, rinse in a bowl of cold water and squeeze dry in a clean cloth or paper towels. Mix in a large bowl with the freshly mashed potatoes. Add the crushed onion, beaten egg, flour, melted butter and seasonings. The potato mixture must be cooked immediately or it will discolor. Drop spoonfuls of the mixture on a lightly greased frying pan, flatten slightly with a spatula, and cook until golden brown on both sides, 3–4 minutes on each side. Serve immediately.

Serves 4–5.

Boxty, like colcannon, is a traditional Irish dish. Serve with ham and eggs, bacon, or green vegetables.

COLCANNON

1 pound kale, cabbage or Brussels sprouts
1 bunch scallions, 1 leek or 1 onion
½ cup milk
1 pound potatoes
4 tablespoons butter
salt and black pepper

Cook the green vegetable in a little rapidly boiling water. Drain well and chop. Chop the scallions, leek or onion and cook over low heat in the milk in a small, covered pan until tender. Put aside. Cook the potatoes, drain and dry over low heat. Make a puree and beat in the milk and onion mixture. Stir in the chopped greens. Mix in the butter and plenty of salt and black pepper. Beat well until very hot and well-mixed. Excellent with sausages or boiled bacon. This is also good made in a frying pan. Omit the milk and cook the scallions in water. Drain the scallions. Make a dry purée of potatoes and mix with the onions and greens. Season well. Heat the butter in a frying pan and spread in the mixture, flattening with a spatula. Cook gently until well browned underneath, about 30 minutes. Turn out on a flat dish and cut in wedges like a cake. Serve with fried ham and eggs or grilled bacon.
　　Serves 4.

POTATO PASTE

1 cup water
5 tablespoons butter
1½ cups flour
3 eggs
1½ cups mashed potatoes
(freshly cooked and dried over low heat)
salt and black pepper
nutmeg

Boil the butter and water in a large saucepan. When the butter has melted, take it off the heat and add the flour. Stir constantly until it makes a thick smooth paste. Break in the eggs one at a time, and beat each one in until the mixture is smooth and comes away from the sides of the pan. Beat in the hot mashed potatoes until mixture is smooth. Season with salt and black pepper and grated nutmeg to taste. Leave to cool. Refrigerate overnight if possible, or at least for a few hours.

Use for gnocchi, potato cakes or potato scones.

POTATO SCONES

---

potato paste (page 92)
3 tablespoons chopped fresh herbs
or
½ cup grated cheese

Make up the paste and add the herbs or cheese. Form into flat, round cakes, about ¾ inch thick, and cook on a very hot, lightly greased griddle or frying pan until golden brown on both sides.
Serves 4.

GNOCCHI

---

potato paste

Make the paste and form into small ovals on a floured board. Bring a large pan of water to a boil and drop in the ovals in batches. Simmer gently for 5 minutes, then lift out with a slotted spoon and drain on a cloth while cooking another batch. Prepare thick tomato sauce (page 143) and pour over the gnocchi. Serve in a shallow dish.
Serves 4.

POTATO CAKES

---

potato paste

Make the paste and form into small round flat cakes on a floured board. Either fry them in butter or bacon fat until browned on both sides, or bake at 375—400 degrees on a buttered baking sheet until lightly risen and browned, about 10—15 minutes. Good with bacon and eggs, or eaten hot with butter.
Serves 6.

Makes about 12 cakes.

POTATO PANCAKES

1 pound potatoes
1 medium onion
2 eggs
2 tablespoons flour
salt and black pepper
arachide oil

Grate the potatoes and onion finely. Put them in a bowl and add the beaten eggs. Sprinkle in the flour, stir well and add salt and black pepper to taste. Mix very well. Do not prepare in advance or the mixture will discolor and separate. Heat a layer of oil in a large frying pan or griddle; when it is hot, drop in spoonfuls of the mixture, flattening them into round cakes with a spatula. Cook over moderate heat until nicely browned, about 5 minutes, then turn over and brown the other side. It is sometimes easier to make one huge pancake. This takes longer to cook but does not need constant attention. When the oil is hot, pour the contents of the bowl into the pan and flatten with a spatula. After about 15–20 minutes over a moderate heat, loosen the edges with a spatula to see if the underneath is browned. Invert a flat dish over the pan and turn the pancake out, heat a little more oil in the pan, and slide the pancake back for another 10–15 minutes to brown the other side. When ready to serve, turn out again onto a flat round platter and cut in wedges.
Serves 4–6.

Excellent with cold meat, fried eggs and bacon or ham and eggs.

POTATO SOUFFLE

1 pound potatoes
1 cup milk
½ small onion
1 clove
6 peppercorns
nutmeg
¼ bay leaf
celery salt
2 tablespoons butter
4 eggs
2 tablespoons grated cheese (optional)

Boil the potatoes, drain, and put them through the medium mesh of a vegetable mill or purée in a blender. You should have 2 cups dry purée. Put the milk in a small pan with the seasonings and flavorings. Bring to simmering point, then leave covered at the side of the heat to infuse for 15—20 minutes. Strain the milk and beat it into the purée. Separate the eggs and beat in the yolks. Beat the egg whites until stiff and fold in. Pour the mixture into a buttered soufflé dish and sprinkle the grated cheese over the top, if liked. Bake at 400 degrees for 20 minutes or at 350 degrees for 25 minutes.
Serves 6.

SOUFFLED POTATOES

1½ pounds Idaho potatoes, cooked
3 eggs
about 2 tablespoons thin cream
2 ounces grated Parmesan
or
Gruyēre cheese
salt and black pepper

Make a dry purée with the potatoes and beat in the yolks of the eggs. Add enough cream to make a smooth thick cream. Beat in the cheese, and season highly with salt and black pepper, bearing in mind the bland mass of egg whites still to be incorporated. Just before cooking, beat the egg whites until stiff and fold in. Have a pan of deep fat heated to a temperature of about 360 degrees. Drop spoonfuls of the potato mixture in, about a teaspoon at a time, but do not put in more than will float freely without crowding. Cook until golden brown on the underneath, about 3—4 minutes, then turn them over with a slotted spoon and brown on the other side. Drain on paper towels while you cook another batch; remove quickly to a hot dish and serve as soon as possible.
Serves 4.

Nutmeg can be substituted for the cheese.

BUBBLE AND SQUEAK

½ pound mashed potatoes
½ pound cooked cabbage or kale
4 tablespoons butter
salt and black pepper

Mix the mashed potatoes and the chopped greens in a bowl. Melt half the butter and stir into the mixture. Season well with plenty of salt and black pepper. Melt the remaining butter in a heavy frying pan and when it is hot, pile in the potato and cabbage mixture. Flatten with a spatula, and cook over a low heat until very hot and browned on the underneath, about 25 minutes. Turn out on a flat dish and serve.

Serves 3—4.

CHAMP

3 cups hot mashed potatoes
1 bunch scallions
½ cup milk
4 tablespoons butter
salt and black pepper

Cook the chopped onions in the milk in a small pan until soft. Drain them, keeping back the milk. Mix the chopped onions into the hot potatoes and beat in the butter in small pieces. Add enough of the milk to make a creamy purée and season well with salt and black pepper. Beat over gentle heat until smooth. To prepare this Irish dish traditionally, the butter should be melted and poured into a well in the middle of the potatoes.

Serves 4.

FRIED POTATOES

oil
½ pound peeled Idaho potatoes

This is particularly good when made with the fat of a duck or goose, or good beef dripping. Peel the raw potatoes and cut them in half, then slice each half thinly and evenly. Heat enough fat in a heavy frying pan to cover the bottom to the thickness of about ½ inch, and when it is very hot put in the sliced potatoes. Cook them over a moderate heat for about 30 minutes—the exact timing will depend on the thickness of the slices—turning them occasionally with a spatula so that the top ones go to the bottom to brown. When all are browned and tender throughout, sprinkle them with salt and a little finely chopped parsley and serve.

Serves 3—4.

CARROT RISOTTO

1 onion
5 tablespoons butter
4 strips bacon
1 cup rice
6 ounces small carrots
3¾ cups chicken stock, hot
black pepper
1 ounce freshly grated Parmesan cheese

Chop the onions and cut the carrots into thin slices. Melt 4 tablespoons butter in a skillet and cook the onions until soft. Add the chopped bacon and cook until golden. Stir in the rice. Add ½ the boiling stock. Add the carrots. Cook gently until the liquid has been absorbed, then add ½ remaining stock, also boiling. Add the remaining stock as the rice gets dry enough to need it; all the stock should be absorbed by the time the rice is cooked. Season with black pepper and dot with the remaining butter. Top with cheese.
    Serves 4 as a main course.

RISI E BISI

1 onion
½ cup butter
2 ounces bacon or prosciutto
1 cup rice
3¾ cups chicken stock
2 cups shelled peas
or
1 pound frozen *petits pois*
1 ounce freshly grated Parmesan cheese
salt and black pepper

Chop the onion finely and cook in 4 tablespoons butter until soft. Chop the bacon and add to the onion. Stir until lightly colored. Add the washed and drained rice, stir well. Heat the stock until almost boiling and pour on half of it. Add the peas and simmer gently until the rice is cooked, adding more stock by degrees. When the rice is tender all the stock should have been absorbed. Season with salt and black pepper. Pour into a serving dish, sprinkle with grated Parmesan cheese and dot with the remaining butter.
    Serves 4.

CAULIFLOWER WITH RICE

1 small cauliflower
¾ cup rice
½ pound sliced ham
3 tablespoons butter
2 tablespoons flour
½ cup milk
¼ pound grated Cheddar cheese
¼ cup cream
salt and black pepper

Cut the cauliflower into sprigs and cook in a small amount of boiling salted water until tender, about 10–15 minutes. Drain, reserving the liquid, and keep warm. Cook the rice and drain. Chop the ham. Melt the butter and add the flour, stirring to make a *roux*. Blend ½ cup of the reserved cooking liquid with the milk, warm, and add to the *roux*. Add the grated cheese to the mixture and stir until smooth. Season to taste, and add the cream. Arrange the rice around the edges of a round shallow dish or use a ring mold. Lay the sprigs of cauliflower in the center with the chopped ham filling up the crevices. Pour half the sauce over the center of the dish. Serve the remaining sauce separately. Place in a low oven for 10 minutes to heat through.
     Serves 4.

GREEN RICE

1 cup rice
½ pound frozen spinach purée
4 tablespoons butter
1 clove garlic or 1 small onion
1½ ounces grated Parmesan cheese
salt and black pepper
grated nutmeg

Boil the rice and drain. Leave in a low oven or plate warmer for 15 minutes to dry. Mince the garlic or onion and cook gently in half the butter without allowing it to brown. Cook the spinach purée and drain; dry out as much as possible by stirring over very gentle heat. Stir the onion and remaining butter into the spinach purée, season well with salt, black pepper and a little grated nutmeg. Mix with the rice and pour into a shallow serving dish. Sprinkle with the grated cheese.

Serves 4.

POTATO CAKE WITH LEEKS

2 leeks
3 cups freshly mashed potatoes
4 tablespoons butter
salt and black pepper

Slice the leeks and cook in 3 tablespoons butter until they are soft. Mix with the mashed potatoes, adding salt and black pepper to taste. Melt the remaining 1 tablespoon butter in a frying pan and when it is hot, pile in the potato and leek mixture. Spread into a pan with a spatula and flatten. Cook gently until brown on underside, about 25—30 minutes. Invert on a plate and cut into wedges to serve.

Serves 4—6.

Two sliced onions can be substituted for the leeks. Good served with fried eggs and bacon.

BAKED SWEET POTATOES

1 medium-sized sweet potato per person
butter
salt and black pepper

Scrub under running water and leave to dry. Heat the oven to 400 degrees, and put the potatoes on the middle rack. Allow 45—60 minutes, testing to see if they are done by squeezing them gently with a cloth. Serve exactly like ordinary baked potatoes, with butter, salt and black pepper.

Sweet potatoes are more suitable than yams for this as their flesh is of a fluffier consistency, but yams may be substituted.

SWEET POTATO PUREE

1½ pounds sweet potatoes
salt and black pepper
4 tablespoons butter
½ cup cream
chopped parsley

Peel the potatoes and cut in pieces. Cover with lightly salted water and cook till tender. Drain very well and dry out by stirring for a few minutes over gentle heat. Push through the medium mesh of the vegetable mill and return to the clean pan. Stir in the butter and cream, and add salt and black pepper to taste. Pour into a serving dish and sprinkle with chopped parsley.
    Serves 4—5.

Do not attempt to make this purée with yams, as they are too moist.

RÖSTI

1½ pounds potatoes
½ cup butter
salt and black pepper

Boil the potatoes in their skins. When cool enough to handle, peel them and slice them thinly or grate coarsely. Heat the butter in a heavy frying pan and put in the potatoes, adding salt and black pepper. Stir them in the hot butter, then press into a flat cake and leave for 25—30 minutes. Invert on a flat dish to serve.
    Serves 4—5.

THREE-VEGETABLE PUREE

1 pound potatoes
1 pound parsnips
heart of a green cabbage, about 1 pound
4 tablespoons butter
salt and black pepper

Boil the potatoes until tender and drain. Push through the medium mesh of a vegetable mill. Peel the parsnips and cut in pieces. Boil until tender and push through the same mesh as the potatoes. Cut the cabbage heart in quarters, remove the inner core and slice the rest. Cook until just tender in boiling salted water. Drain it well and chop finely. Mix the potato and parsnip purée in a heavy pan over a gentle heat and stir in the chopped cabbage. Put in the butter, cut in small pieces, and season well with plenty of salt and black pepper. Serve very hot.

Serves 6.

Excellent with boiled ham or bacon.

GRATIN DAUPHINOIS

1½ pounds potatoes
1 large egg
2 cups milk
1 clove garlic, minced
1¼ cups grated Gruyère or Fontina cheese (optional)
salt and black pepper
nutmeg

Peel the potatoes and slice them thinly and evenly. Mix the beaten egg, milk, garlic and cheese together. Add the sliced potatoes. Season to taste with the nutmeg, salt and black pepper. Pour into the buttered gratin dish and bake for 60 minutes at 350 degrees.

Serves 4–6.

Gratin Savoyard can be made from this recipe by substituting chicken stock for the cheese.

POTATO CROQUETTES

1½ pounds potatoes, cooked
2 egg yolks
salt and black pepper
nutmeg
1 egg
fine dry bread crumbs
butter and light oil

Make the potatoes into a dry purée. Beat in the egg yolks, one at a time. Season with salt, black pepper and a little grated nutmeg. Spread out on a floured board and when cooled divide into 15 equal parts, and form into rolls. Coat the rolls with lightly beaten egg, and roll in the bread crumbs. Heat the butter and oil and fry until golden, turning on all sides. Drain on paper towels. Serve as soon as possible.

Serves 4—5.

HASHED POTATOES

---

2 pounds potatoes
1 Spanish onion
salt and black pepper
2 tablespoons butter
2 tablespoons olive oil

Preheat the oven to 400 degrees while you scrub the potatoes. Bake 45—60 minutes until soft when tested with a fork. Peel and grate them coarsely. Grate the onion finely and mix lightly with the potatoes, seasoning with salt and black pepper. Heat the butter and oil in a frying pan until very hot. Add the potatoes. Flatten with a spatula and cook over a low flame for 30—40 minutes, lifting the edges now and then to make sure it is not burning. Invert on a flat dish to serve. It should be brown and crusty on top.

Serves 4.

Serve with fried eggs and bacon, fried tomatoes, grilled steaks or chops.

VEGETABLE COUSCOUS

¾ pound precooked couscous
6 cups chicken stock
6 small onions
4 leeks, sliced
4 carrots, sliced
4 zucchini, sliced
6 tomatoes, peeled
2 stalks celery, sliced
salt and black pepper
1 teaspoon coriander
½ pound chickpeas, presoaked and cooked
¼ teaspoon saffron

Put the couscous in a bowl and pour 2 cups cold water over it. Leave to ab-sorb. Put the chicken stock in a large pot, add the whole onions and bring slowly to a boil. When the stock reaches a boil, add the leeks, carrots and celery. Put the couscous in a muslin-lined strainer, place in the pot and cover. Keep boiling gently for 30 minutes, then remove the strainer and add the unpeeled zucchini. Season well. Stir the couscous, and break up any lumps with a fork. Replace and cover the pan. After 10 minutes, add the whole tomatoes. Cook another 5 minutes after it returns to a boil and remove from the heat. Turn the couscous into a heated dish and break up with a fork. Add the saffron and chickpeas to the vegetables. Pour the vegetables and stock into a tureen and serve the couscous separately, gar-nished with a few of the vegetables.

Serves 8.

To make a heartier meal, cook a jointed chicken with the vegetables.

[10]

Salads

ARABIC SALAD

---

1 Arab or Greek loaf bread (pitta)
1 large cucumber
4 tomatoes
1 onion, sliced
2 cloves garlic
2 tablespoons chopped parsley
2 tablespoons chopped mint
olive oil
1 large lemon or 2 small ones
salt and black pepper
1 heart of romaine lettuce

Split the bread open and leave overnight to dry, or place in the sun for a few hours. Chop the peeled cucumber and tomatoes into similar sized squares. Break up the bread into small pieces. Put the bread in the bottom of a large bowl and cover with the tomatoes, the cucumber, the sliced onion, the crushed garlic and the chopped herbs. Squeeze the lemon and measure the juice. Pour it over the vegetables and add twice as much olive oil. Chill in the refrigerator for 3–4 hours. Before serving, chop the lettuce and add to the mixture.

Serves 6.

ARABIC PARSLEY SALAD

1 cup crushed wheat *(burghul)*
1½ cups finely chopped parsley
½ cup finely chopped mint
1 bunch scallions
2 large tomatoes, peeled
½ cup olive oil
½ cup lemon juice
salt and black pepper

Soak the crushed wheat (obtainable from health food shops) for 1 hour in cold water; drain and squeeze to press out as much water as possible. Put the crushed wheat in a large bowl and mix with the chopped parsley and mint. Chop the scallions and the peeled tomatoes and mix with the crushed wheat. Add the lemon juice and oil gradually, beating in with a wooden spoon. Add salt and black pepper to taste, and more oil or lemon as required. Serve on a large platter with a border of sliced tomatoes, and a bowl of small crisp lettuce leaves with which to eat it.
    Serves 6.

An unusual salad, except in Lebanon where it is almost a national dish, this is refreshing and very nutritious.

BEET SALAD

1 pound small beets
salt and black pepper
olive oil
white wine vinegar

Cut the leaves off the beets and reserve them. Scrub the beets and put in cold water to cover. Add salt, bring to a boil and cook until tender. Chop the leaves and cook separately for 4–5 minutes in a little boiling salted water. Drain. When the beets are cooked, drain them and slice thickly. Lay on a flat dish, sprinkle with salt and black pepper, lay the chopped leaves over the top and pour over olive oil and vinegar (3 parts oil to 1 part vinegar) to taste. Serve before it has completely cooled.
    Serves 4.

BLACK RADISH AND CUCUMBER SALAD

1 black radish
1 cucumber
salt and black pepper
3 tablespoons sunflower-seed oil
1 tablespoon white wine vinegar

Peel the radish and the cucumber, and grate both coarsely. Mix in a bowl, season with salt and black pepper. Mix the oil and vinegar. Add dressing just before serving.
Serves 4.

BROCCOLI SALAD

1 pound broccoli
olive oil
lemon juice
salt and black pepper

Cook the broccoli in boiling salted water, or steam it, until just tender. Drain it and lay on a flat dish. While it is still hot, pour over it olive oil and lemon juice—roughly 3 parts oil to 1 part lemon juice—and sprinkle with salt and black pepper.
Serves 4.

CELERIAC REMOULADE

1 pound celeriac

Sauce rémoulade:
2 hard-boiled egg yolks
2 raw egg yolks
salt and pepper
1 tablespoon Dijon mustard
2 tablespoons tarragon vinegar
or
2 tablespoons white wine vinegar
1¼ cups olive oil or sunflower oil
½ cup sour cream (optional)

Scrub the celeriac well, cut into thin strips, drop into boiling water and parboil it for 5 minutes. Make the sauce: put the hard-boiled egg yolks into a bowl and mash to a paste. Add the raw egg yolks, and beat until a smooth mixture is obtained. Add the vinegar gradually and blend very carefully. Then add the oil drop by drop, stirring constantly. Taste and adjust seasoning. The sauce should be strongly flavored with mustard and vinegar. Stir in the cream and mix with the celeriac.

Serves 4–6.

This classic French hors d'oeuvre can also be made with raw celery.

CHICKPEA SALAD

½ pound chickpeas
salt and black pepper
1 clove garlic
1 lemon
½ cup olive oil
2 tablespoons finely chopped parsley

Soak the peas overnight. Put them in a saucepan and cover generously with cold water. Bring slowly to a boil and simmer gently until tender—about 2 hours. Add salt only towards the end of the cooking. Drain the peas when they are soft enough to crush between your fingers, put them in a bowl and add salt and black pepper to taste. Stir in the juice of 1 lemon, a crushed clove of garlic and about ½ cup olive oil. Sprinkle with chopped parsley and serve before they have completely cooled.

Serves 4–5.

CUCUMBER AND TOMATO RING

1 cucumber
½ pound tomatoes
1 package gelatin
2 tablespoons lemon juice
1 tablespoon white wine vinegar
1/8 teaspoon chili sauce

Filling:
¼ teaspoon sugar
4 tablespoons cream
¼ pound cream cheese
4 tablespoons mixed chopped parsley,
chives or chervil or dill

Grate the peeled cucumber, reserving any juice. Peel, deseed and chop the tomatoes, reserving any juice. Dissolve the gelatin in ½ cup cold water for 10 minutes, pour on 1 cup boiling water and mix. Add the lemon juice, vinegar, chili sauce, sugar and the juice from the cucumber and tomatoes. When cool add the cucumber and tomato, mix well, and pour into a ring mold and chill. To make the filling, mix the cream and cream cheese and stir in the herbs. Chill until firm and then form into balls. Turn out the jelly on a flat dish and fill the center with the cream cheese balls.
Serves 4–6.

CUCUMBER MOUSSE

¼ pound cream cheese
½ cup cream, sour cream or yoghurt
½ ounce package gelatin
½ cup chicken stock
1 cucumber
1 teaspoon lemon juice
salt and black pepper

Beat together the cream cheese and the cream, sour cream or yoghurt until smooth. (Use cream for a richer dish, yoghurt for a simple unfattening one.) Melt the gelatin in the stock. Grate the peeled cucumber and mix it into the cheese mixture. Add the lemon juice, salt and black pepper to taste. Pour the melted gelatin through a strainer into the mixture and stir thoroughly. When well mixed, pour into a soufflé dish or mold and chill.
Serves 4.

CUCUMBER WITH YOGHURT

1 cucumber
2 cups yoghurt
salt and black pepper
2 large cloves garlic
2 tablespoons chopped mint or chives

Empty the yoghurt into a large bowl and beat with a wooden spoon until smooth. Crush 2 large cloves garlic and mix into the yoghurt with salt and black pepper to taste. Peel the cucumber and cut into thin slices. Mix into the yoghurt. Chill for several hours before serving, then sprinkle with the chopped herbs at the last minute. A very popular Middle-Eastern dish, this salad is served sprinkled with dried mint, which most families make themselves. It is also delicious with fresh mint or chives.

Serves 6.

The quantities can easily be doubled for a buffet supper, or halved for a side dish to eat with curry, in which case the herbs should be omitted. A very delicious cooling dish that goes well with rich beef stews, roast lamb, or heavily spiced dishes.

EGG AND TOMATO SALAD

6 hard-boiled eggs
4 large tomatoes or 6 medium ones
½ Spanish onion
olive oil
vinegar
salt and black pepper
finely chopped parsley or chives

Chop the eggs. Peel the tomatoes and cut them in similar sized pieces, discarding seeds and juice. Slice the onion very fine and divide each slice into rings. Mix the eggs, tomatoes and onion with enough olive oil and vinegar to moisten, 3 parts oil to 1 part vinegar. Season to taste with salt and black pepper, and serve in a bowl. Garnish with fresh herbs.

Serves 4.

EGGPLANT MEZA

2 large eggplants
½ cup tahini
1 cup lemon juice
salt and pepper
2 cloves garlic, crushed
1–2 tablespoons olive oil
finely chopped parsley

Bake the eggplants for 45 minutes at 350 degrees. Cut in half and scoop out the flesh. Purée in a blender or a vegetable mill. Beat in the tahini and lemon juice alternately. Stir in the crushed garlic and add salt and pepper to taste. Pour onto a plate and make swirls in the top. Pour a dribble of olive oil over the top and sprinkle with parsley. Serve with hot Arabic bread (pitta).

Serves 6.

Tahini, or sesame seed paste, can be purchased in a health food store.

EGGPLANT PUREE

3 large eggplants
1 clove garlic, crushed
1 tablespoon onion juice
2 tablespoons olive oil
1 tablespoon lemon juice
salt and black pepper
½ tablespoon very finely chopped parsley

Bake the eggplants at 350 degrees for about 45 minutes. When they are soft, cut them in half and scoop out the flesh. Put it through the medium mesh vegetable mill or purée in a blender. Add the crushed garlic and the onion juice. Stir in the olive oil and add about half as much lemon juice, just enough to sharpen the purée. Add salt and black pepper to taste. Chill several hours. Sprinkle with chopped parsley before serving. Serve with toast or homemade bread.

Serves 4.

EGGPLANT SALAD

2 eggplants
1 Spanish onion
4 tomatoes
salt and black pepper
olive oil
vinegar

Cook the eggplants in boiling water for 20 minutes, then drain and cool. Chop the onion and skin and chop the tomatoes. When cool enough to handle, peel the eggplants and chop the flesh. Mix all the vegetables together, season with salt and black pepper, and stir in enough oil and vinegar to moisten thoroughly, allowing roughly 3 parts oil to 1 part vinegar.

Serves 4.

EGG SALAD

---

6 hard-boiled eggs
1 head lettuce, round or romaine
1 bunch scallions or 1 medium onion
4 tomatoes
½ cucumber
6 new potatoes

Dressing:
6 tablespoons olive oil
2 tablespoons white wine vinegar
salt and black pepper

Slice the eggs thickly. Shred the tender, inside leaves of the lettuce. Slice the scallions or onion thinly. Peel and slice the tomatoes and cucumber. Boil the potatoes in their skins, cool and peel them, then slice thickly. Make a bed of shredded lettuce on a flat dish. Arrange the sliced eggs, tomatoes, onions, cucumber and potatoes in rows. To make a dressing, add the olive oil to the vinegar, stirring constantly. Season to taste with salt and pepper. Pour over the salad just before serving.

Serves 4.

GREEK SALAD

½ cucumber
½ pound tomatoes
1 large green pepper or 2 small ones
1 Spanish onion
6 ounces feta cheese

6 tablespoons olive oil
2 tablespoons white wine vinegar
salt and black pepper
1 teaspoon dried marjoram or oregano

Peel the cucumber and cut in slices, not too thin. Peel the tomatoes, and cut in quarters or eighths. Remove the pith and seeds from the pepper and cut in strips. Slice the onion thinly. Mix all the vegetables in a bowl. Mix the oil and vinegar with salt and black pepper, and pour over the salad. Dice the cheese and scatter over the salad. Sprinkle the marjoram over all and mix well. Alternatively serve 3—4 tablespoons dried marjoram in a little bowl, and let each person add it according to taste.

Serves 4—5.

Another version of this salad is made by crumbling the cheese into the dressing and mixing with the salad. In this case, ¼ pound cheese will be enough.

GUACAMOLE

2 large avocadoes
½ pound tomatoes
1 bunch scallions
1 green pepper
2 green chilis
salt and black pepper
2 tablespoons lemon juice
1 tablespoon olive oil

Peel the avocadoes, cut them in half, remove the stones and chop the flesh in small dice. Skin the tomatoes and chop them finely. Chop the bulb part of the scallions. Cut the pepper in half, remove the pith and seeds, and chop in small dice. Blanch the chilis (this can be done when skinning the tomatoes) and chop very finely, removing all the seeds. Mix together and season with salt and black pepper. Stir in the lemon juice and olive oil.

Serves 4.

Serve alone as a first course or a salad, or as a filling for pancakes, the center of a tomato jelly ring (see p. 127) or a filling for stuffed eggs, adding some of the chopped egg yolks for garnish.

HOMUS

1 pound chickpeas
salt and black pepper
1 cup tahini (sesame seed paste,
obtainable in health food stores)
1 cup lemon juice
3 large cloves garlic
approximately 2 tablespoons olive oil
or
sesame seed oil
finely chopped parsley
red pepper or paprika

Soak the chickpeas overnight, then cover them with fresh cold water in a deep pan. Bring very slowly to a boil and simmer until soft when crushed between the fingers. This should take about 2 hours, but it may be longer. Replenish the water as necessary. When cooked, drain the peas and purée in a blender or a vegetable mill. Stir in tahini and lemon juice alternately. Crush the garlic and stir in, and add salt and black pepper to taste. When mixture is smooth, pour onto a large plate. Make a few swirls on the top, and pour a film of olive or sesame seed oil over it. Sprinkle with a little finely chopped parsley, paprika or a dusting of red pepper. Serve with hot Arabic bread (pitta).

Serves 10–12.

Homus keeps well in the refrigerator, covered with an oiled piece of saran wrap.

MIXED BEAN SALAD I

½ pound dried haricot beans
¾ pound string beans
olive oil
white wine vinegar
salt and black pepper
1 onion

Soak the dried beans for 1 hour, then cook until tender in simmering un-salted water. Add salt when the cooking is almost over. Cook the string beans until tender, drain them and cut into 1-inch pieces. Mix the two kinds of beans together while still hot, and stir in enough oil to moisten thoroughly without making a pool in the bottom of the bowl. Add white wine vinegar to taste, or in the proportion of 3 parts oil to 1 part vinegar. Season with plenty of salt and black pepper. Cut the onion in half, slice finely and divide each slice into rings. Mix with the beans and serve as soon as it has cooled.

Serves 6.

MIXED SALAD

1 head lettuce
4 new potatoes
¼ pound string beans
2 large tomatoes
2 hard-boiled eggs

Dressing:
salt and black pepper
¼ teaspoon Dijon mustard
5 tablespoons olive oil
1½ tablespoons white wine vinegar
1 clove garlic (optional)

Wash and dry the lettuce and put the leaves in a large bowl. Boil the potatoes in their skins, and skin them as soon as they are cool enough to handle. Boil the beans until just tender and cut in 1-inch pieces. Cut the tomatoes in wedges. Cut the eggs in quarters. Arrange all the ingredients on top of the lettuce. To make the dressing, put a pinch of salt and pepper in a cup with ¼ teaspoon mustard. Stir in the oil, then blend with the vinegar. Put a whole peeled clove of garlic in the cup and leave until time to serve. Then remove the garlic, pour the dressing over the salad and mix well.

Serves 4.

With the addition of an 8-ounce tin of tuna fish, drained and broken into chunks; 6 anchovy fillets, drained of their oil and chopped; and 8 black olives, this becomes *salade niçoise*.

SWEET PEPPER SALAD

2 large red peppers
2 large green peppers
salt and black pepper
2 tablespoons olive oil
1 tablespoon lemon juice
or
white wine vinegar

Put the peppers under a broiler and cook until all sides are blackened and blistered. Remove from heat and cool slightly. When they are cool enough to handle, remove the skin with a small sharp knife. Cut away the stalk and remove the inner pith and seeds. Cut in thin strips. Mix the two colored peppers in a dish and sprinkle with salt and black pepper. Pour on oil and lemon juice or vinegar, according to taste. Leave for 30 minutes, then serve.
    Serves 4 as an accompaniment to other dishes.

Peeling peppers is a lengthy business, so do not attempt it in large quantities. In any case this excellent salad is one to be eaten in small amounts, with either one or two other hors d'oeuvres.

SUMMER SALAD

1 head lettuce
1 cucumber
1½ pounds green peas in the pod
or
¼ pound shelled
or
frozen peas
½ teaspoon sugar
salt and black pepper
1 tablespoon white wine vinegar
2 tablespoons thin cream
2 tablespoons olive oil

Wash the lettuce leaves and drain; pat dry. Cook the peas and drain; moisten with a little olive oil while still hot. Peel the cucumber and cut it in batons (cut into 9 stick-shaped pieces) and into 2-inch slices. To make the dressing put the sugar, salt and black pepper in a small bowl, pour in the vinegar and mix to dissolve the seasonings. Add the cream and the olive oil and beat well. Arrange the lettuce leaves in a salad bowl. Put the cucumber on top and scatter the peas over, or pile them in the center. Pour on the dressing at the last moment and mix well.

Serves 6.

An excellent accompaniment to cold salmon trout.

CARROT SALAD

½ pound new carrots
½ cup yoghurt
2 tablespoons orange juice

Shred or grate the carrots as finely as possible. Put the yoghurt in a small bowl and mix until smooth. Add to the carrots. Stir in the orange juice. Do not try using old carrots for this dish, as they are too coarse.

Serves 4.

CUCUMBER AND CHEESE SALAD

1 cup cream cheese
3 tablespoons lemon juice
2 tablespoons sunflower-seed oil
½ cucumber, diced
salt and black pepper
4 tablespoons chopped chives

Mash the cheese with the lemon juice until it forms a smooth cream, then beat in the oil. Peel the cucumber and cut in very small dice. Mix into the cheese and season with salt and black pepper to taste, and more lemon juice if necessary. Mix in the chives and chill. To serve, pile on crisp lettuce leaves, or use as a stuffing for tomatoes or a filling for a tomato aspic ring.

Serves 4.

CUCUMBER AND SOUR CREAM SALAD

1 cucumber
1 cup sour cream
2 tablespoons tarragon vinegar
1 teaspoon sugar
½ teaspoon sea salt
2 tablespoons chopped chives
or
dill or scallions

Peel and slice the cucumber. Sprinkle with salt and leave to drain. Pat dry. Mix the other ingredients, beating until smooth. Combine with the cucumber and sprinkle the chives or other garnish over the top. Chill.
Serves 4–6.

SIMPLE LETTUCE SALAD

1 head lettuce
lemon juice
sugar

Simply pile the dried lettuce leaves in a bowl and sprinkle with lemon juice and sugar to taste.
Serves 4.

EASY TOMATO SALAD

1 pound tomatoes
salt and black pepper
sugar

Skin the tomatoes and leave them whole. Cut an X-shaped incision in the top, and pull out the central core. Leave upside down for a little while to allow all the juice and seeds to drain away. Arrange right side up on a plate and sprinkle lightly with salt, sugar and black pepper. Do not add any dressing, but serve quite plainly. They make an excellent accompaniment to dishes dressed with olive oil or cream dressings.
Serves 4.

LENTIL VINAIGRETTE

½ pound cooked brown lentils
1 small onion
2 ounces bacon strips
salt and black pepper
3 tablespoons olive oil
1 tablespoon white wine vinegar

Chop the onion finely and mix with the lentils. Fry the bacon till crisp, then drain and crumble or chop into small pieces. Mix with the lentils. Season with salt and freshly ground black pepper and pour the oil and vinegar over the mixture. The bacon can be omitted or replaced by slices of pepperoni or warm sliced frankfurters. This salad is best served warm.

Serves 4.

MIXED AMERICAN SALAD

1 head crisp lettuce
4 tomatoes
¼ pound cooked ham, in one thick slice
¼ pound Gruyère cheese
1 cup croutons

Dressing:
salt and black pepper
5 tablespoons olive oil
1½ tablespoons white wine vinegar

Wash and dry the lettuce, and put the leaves in a bowl. Cut the unskinned tomatoes in wedges and add to the bowl. Cut the ham and cheese in cubes. Scatter both over the lettuce and tomatoes. Add the croutons. To make the dressing, mix the seasonings and the wine vinegar. Add the olive oil slowly, stirring constantly. Add to salad and toss lightly just before serving.

Serves 4.

Homemade croutons are easily made by dicing day-old bread and sautéing in butter.

ORANGE AND WATERCRESS SALAD

3 oranges
2 bunches watercress
salt and black pepper
4 tablespoons sunflower-seed oil
1½ tablespoons lemon juice

Peel the oranges removing all the white pith. Cut in thin slices. Divide the watercress into sprigs; wash and dry well. Mix the two together, seasoning with salt and black pepper. Pour on the oil and lemon juice and mix well. Serves 3–4.

LETTUCE, BACON AND MUSHROOM SALAD

4 ounces bacon strips
4 ounces raw mushrooms
1 head lettuce
salt and black pepper
3 tablespoons olive oil
1 tablespoon white wine vinegar

Fry the bacon until crisp; drain. Chop or break into small pieces. Slice the mushrooms; tear the lettuce leaves into pieces. Mix the three ingredients in a bowl. Make a dressing with the oil and vinegar and salt and black pepper, and pour over the salad. Serves 4.

HOT POTATO SALAD

1½ pounds new or waxy potatoes
1 medium onion
salt and black pepper
¼ pound bacon strips
2 tablespoons white wine vinegar
2 tablespoons finely chopped parsley

Boil the potatoes in their skins until tender and drain. Remove the skins as soon as possible and cut into thick slices. Chop the onion finely and mix with the potatoes, seasoning with salt and black pepper. Dice the bacon and fry slowly until crisp. Drain, then mix with the salad. Pour the vinegar into the bacon fat remaining in the pan, reheat carefully as it may froth, and pour over the salad. Mix well and serve at once.

Serves 4.

POTATO SALAD I

1½ pounds new or waxy potatoes
salt and black pepper
1 bunch scallions
or
1 small onion
3 tablespoons chopped chives
3 tablespoons chopped chervil or parsley
4 tablespoons olive oil
1 tablespoon white wine vinegar

Boil the potatoes in their skins and drain. Remove the skins as soon as possible, and cut the potatoes in fairly thick slices, trying not to break them. Slice the scallions. Put the potatoes in a bowl and scatter the onions and the herbs over them. Season with salt and black pepper and pour on the oil and vinegar.

Serves 4.

Do not make this dish too far in advance; if it is left too long, the oil will be absorbed and more must be added.

POTATO SALAD II

1½ pounds new or waxy potatoes
½ cup cream
salt and black pepper
1 bunch scallions
4–6 tablespoons chopped parsley and chives

Boil the potatoes in their skins and drain. Remove the skins as soon as possible and slice the potatoes into a shallow bowl. Beat the cream with the salt and black pepper and pour over the sliced potatoes. Lift carefully with a spatula trying not to break them. Mix in half the herbs and scatter the rest over the top. Serve within an hour if possible.

Serves 4.

RADISH AND CUCUMBER SALAD

1 bunch (about ¼ pound) radishes
½ cucumber
¼ cup thin cream
¼ cup yoghurt
salt and black pepper
¼ teaspoon sugar
2–3 tablespoons lemon juice

Trim the radishes, peel the cucumber, and slice both very thinly. Mix the two together. Put the salt, black pepper and sugar in a small bowl and mix with the cream and yoghurt. Add lemon juice to taste and pour over the radishes and cucumber. Mix well.

Serves 4.

RICE SALAD WITH PEPPERS AND PEAS

1 cup rice
salt and black pepper
grated nutmeg
1 cup cream
juice of ½ lemon
1 large red pepper
½ pound frozen peas

Cook the rice, drain and season while still hot with salt, black pepper and grated nutmeg. Add the cream and lemon juice. Broil the pepper until the skin has blackened on all sides. Remove the skin and dice the flesh, discarding the seeds. Cook the peas until just tender and drain. Mix the chopped pepper and the peas with the rice.

Serves 6.

RICE SALAD WITH HERBS

1 cup rice
salt and black pepper
grated nutmeg
3 tablespoons olive oil

1 teaspoon white wine vinegar
1 teaspoon tarragon vinegar
4–6 tablespoons chopped fresh herbs
1½ ounces pine kernels

Cook the rice. Drain well. While still hot, add salt, black pepper and grated nutmeg to taste. Stir in the oil and vinegars. When cool, stir in the chopped herbs (e.g. chives, chervil, dill, tarragon, parsley) and the pine nuts, keeping back a little of each to scatter over the top.

Serves 6.

SAFFRON RICE WITH PEAS

1 cup rice
½ teaspoon saffron
2¼ cups chicken stock
1 cup thin cream
1 package frozen peas
lemon juice
salt and black pepper

Cook the rice in the stock with half the saffron. Drain when tender and put in a large bowl. Heat half the cream with the remaining saffron; when well flavored, mix with the rest of the cream and sharpen with lemon juice. Cook the peas and drain. Mix the rice and peas while still hot and add the saffron cream. Mix well and adjust seasoning, adding more lemon juice, salt and black pepper to taste. Leave to cool. A pretty dish for a buffet supper. Do not prepare too long in advance or it will become rather thick and solid.

Serves 6.

SALAD SAN LORENZO

½ pound young spinach
1 avocado
¼ pound bacon strips
1 cup Mozzarella cheese, diced

Dressing:
salt and black pepper
6 tablespoons olive oil
2 tablespoons white wine vinegar

Wash the spinach well, remove the stalks and cut the leaves across in ½-inch strips. Fry the bacon and drain on paper towels. When cool, crumble or chop it. Peel and stone the avocado and cut in slices. Mix the spinach, avocado, bacon and cheese together. Make the dressing and pour over just before serving. Serve immediately.

Serves 4.

SORREL AND LETTUCE SALAD WITH BACON

1 bunch sorrel (about 2 ounces)
1 head romaine lettuce
4 strips streaky bacon
1 tablespoon white wine vinegar
black pepper

Cut the sorrel in thin strips with scissors. Break the lettuce in 2-inch chunks. Mix the sorrel and the lettuce together in a bowl. Chop the bacon and fry very slowly till crisp. Lift out the chopped bacon and add to the salad. Pour the vinegar into the hot fat carefully. Grind some black pepper over it and as soon as it is hot pour it over the salad and serve immediately.

Serves 4.

SPINACH AND BACON SALAD I

½ pound spinach
¼ pound bacon strips
3 tablespoons olive oil
1 tablespoon white wine vinegar
salt and black pepper

Cut the stalks off the spinach with scissors. Wash the leaves very well and drain. Toss in a soft cloth to get rid of as much moisture as possible, then cut them in thin strips. Fry the bacon and drain on soft paper. When cool, chop or crumble into small pieces. Mix the spinach and bacon in a bowl, and pour on the *vinaigrette* made with the olive oil and vinegar, and salt and black pepper. No extra flavoring is needed. Serve immediately.

Serves 4.

SPINACH AND BACON SALAD II

Use the same ingredients as for Spinach and Bacon Salad I, but omit the oil. Prepare the spinach beforehand, but fry the bacon at the last moment. After removing the bacon from the pan, crumble it quickly and mix with the spinach while still hot. Carefully pour 1 tablespoon wine vinegar into the pan containing the bacon fat, stir for a moment, then pour it over the salad, mix and serve immediately. This salad must not be allowed to wait, or the fat will cool and congeal.
  Serves 3–4.

SPINACH AND YOGHURT SALAD

1 pound spinach
½ cup yoghurt
1 clove garlic
salt and black pepper

Cook the spinach in a little boiling salted water for about 4–5 minutes. Drain well, squeezing out excess moisture with your hands as soon as the spinach is cool enough to handle. Chop with a long knife on a board. Beat the yoghurt with a wooden spoon until smooth; crush the garlic in a press and mix into the yoghurt. Add salt and black pepper to taste. Mix the yoghurt with the chopped spinach; chill slightly before serving.
  Serves 3–4.

SWEET CORN MAYONNAISE

2 cups fresh, frozen or canned corn
½ cup mayonnaise
½ cup sour cream
salt and black pepper
lemon juice
2 strips bacon

If using fresh corn, allow 6 ears. Cut off the kernels with a sharp knife and cook in a very little lightly salted water until tender, about 4 minutes. Drain and cool. Mix the mayonnaise with the sour cream, and stir into the corn when it has cooled. Add salt and black pepper to taste, also lemon juice. Fry the bacon until crisp, drain and crumble. Scatter over the corn.
  Serves 4.

RED BEAN SALAD

½ pound red kidney beans, cooked or canned
1 celery heart
1 heart of romaine lettuce
6 tablespoons olive oil
2 tablespoons white wine vinegar
2 tablespoons chopped chives

If using canned beans, rinse them well in a colander under running water. Drain and put them in a large bowl. Slice the celery heart and mix with the beans. Slice the lettuce heart in ½-inch pieces and add to the salad. Mix the oil and vinegar with salt and black pepper and pour over the mixture. Scatter the chopped chives over all.
Serves 4–5.

TOMATO AND AVOCADO SALAD

¾ pound tomatoes
2 avocadoes
1 orange
½ lemon

Skin the tomatoes, cut them in half vertically, then slice them. Peel the avocadoes, cut in half and remove the stones. Slice each half to the same thickness as the tomatoes. Mix the two together in a dish. Squeeze the juice of the orange and the half lemon. Pour over the salad and mix. This salad can be dressed with oil and lemon juice, but the fruit juices alone are very refreshing.
Serves 4.

SPANISH SALAD

1 cucumber
1 pound tomatoes
1 small French loaf, 1–2 days old
1 Spanish onion

Dressing:
4 tablespoons olive oil
1½ tablespoons white wine vinegar
salt and black pepper
sugar

Wash the cucumber but do not peel it. Slice it thinly. Peel the tomatoes and slice them thinly. Slice the onion finely and divide each slice into rings. Cut the dry bread in cubes. Arrange the sliced vegetables and bread in layers in a glass bowl. Make the dressing and pour it on. Chill in the refrigerator for several hours before serving.

Serves 4.

This is like a solid version of *gazpacho*, the iced Spanish soup. For a less substantial salad, the bread can be omitted.

TOMATO ASPIC RING

¾ pound tomatoes
1 clove garlic
½ small onion
1 clove
½ bay leaf
1 tablespoon fresh chopped basil
or
½ teaspoon dried basil
Tabasco or other chili sauce
salt and black pepper
½ ounce package gelatin

Skin the raw tomatoes and purée them in the blender. You will need 1½ cups. Pour into a small pan and add all the other ingredients except the gelatin. Bring slowly to a boil, then cover and leave for 20 minutes to infuse the flavors. Melt the gelatin in ¼ cup hot water. Add to the tomato mixture and stir over low heat until melted. Pour through a strainer into a ring mold. Chill for 3—4 hours or overnight. Turn out on a flat platter to serve, and fill the center with cucumber and cheese salad, cold flaked fish in mayonnaise or shredded lettuce with shelled prawns. Pass the mayonnaise separately.

Serves 4—5.

TONNO E FAGIOLI

½ pound dried haricot beans
1 carrot
1 stalk celery
½ bay leaf
olive oil
white wine vinegar
8 ounces tuna fish
salt and black pepper
2 tablespoons chopped parsley

Soak the beans for 3 hours prior to cooking. Cook the beans gently in simmering water with the carrot, celery and bay leaf until they are tender. Add salt towards the end of the cooking. When the beans are tender, drain them and throw away the flavoring vegetables. Put the beans in a large bowl, season to taste, and pour as much olive oil and vinegar as is necessary to moisten the beans well without making a pool in the bottom of the bowl. Season to taste with salt and pepper. Pile the beans onto a plate or platter and put the tuna fish, drained of its oil, on the top. Pour a little fresh olive oil over the tuna, and sprinkle with the chopped parsley.
    Serves 4–5.

To make haricot beans *vinaigrette*, omit the tuna fish and mix raw onion rings with the beans.

WHOLE TOMATOES IN HORSERADISH SAUCE

1½ pounds small, ripe tomatoes

Horseradish sauce:
½ cup mayonnaise
½ cup sour cream
4 tablespoons grated horseradish, fresh if possible
lemon juice

Skin the tomatoes and leave them whole. Chill in the refrigerator while making the sauce. Mix the mayonnaise and the sour cream in a bowl. Stir in the horseradish and add lemon juice to taste. Pile the tomatoes in a pyramid on a plate and spoon the sauce over. Chill in the refrigerator until time to serve.
    Serves 6.

This makes an excellent accompaniment to cold beef dishes.

[11]

Sauces

AIOLI

---

4 cloves garlic
2 egg yolks
salt
1 cup olive oil
1–2 tablespoons white wine vinegar
or
lemon juice

Crush the garlic. Break in the egg yolks and mix into the garlic. Add a pinch of salt. Beat continuously as you add the oil drop by drop. When 1/3 of the oil has been amalgamated, add it more quickly. If the mixture gets too thick, add a little of the vinegar or lemon juice to thin it. When all the oil is used, add more vinegar or lemon to taste. This recipe calls for the genuine Provençal proportion of garlic and is very pungent; for those who prefer a milder version, cut down the garlic to 2 cloves.

Serves 4.

A delicious accompaniment to dishes of plainly boiled vegetables, such as string beans, zucchini, carrots or peas, also hard-boiled eggs, boiled cod or poached chicken, this sauce can be the basis of a whole meal. It is equally good with raw tomatoes, lettuce and cucumber.

LIGHT CURRY SAUCE

2 cups milk
¼ bay leaf
½ small onion
1 clove
salt
6 black peppercorns
2 tablespoons butter
1½ tablespoons flour
1½ tablespoons light curry powder
4 tablespoons cream
lemon juice
cayenne pepper

Put the milk in a small pan with the bay leaf, onion, clove, salt and pepper-corns. Bring to a boil, cover, and leave off the heat for 20 minutes to infuse. Strain and reheat. Melt the butter, stir in the flour and curry powder, and pour in the milk. Stir till smooth and well blended. Simmer for 4 minutes, then add the cream and lemon juice to taste. Add more seasonings as required: cayenne pepper, more curry powder, salt. Add lemon juice to taste.
Serves 4.

This is a light curry sauce in the French manner, so do not be tempted to add too much curry powder; a strong curry would overpower vegetables.

SAUCE HOLLANDAISE

½ cup butter
1 tablespoon white wine vinegar
or
lemon juice
¼ bay leaf
4 black peppercorns
3 egg yolks
salt

Cut the butter in small pieces and melt over low heat. Put the vinegar in a small pan with 3 tablespoons water, the bay leaf and peppercorns. Heat slowly. Break the egg yolks into the top half of a double boiler. Have the water in the bottom pan heating while you beat the yolks for 3 minutes.

When the water reaches the boiling point, turn down the heat so the water simmers. Set pan of eggs over the hot water and continue to beat until they have thickened very slightly. Remove the bay leaf and peppercorns and add the hot vinegar very, very slowly to the eggs. Continue to beat all the time and maintain an even heat. When all the vinegar is added, start to add the butter, beating continuously. Add the butter very slowly. When all the butter is absorbed, taste and add a little salt. The sauce will never become very thick, nor should it be made very hot. It should be served warm, and can be kept warm for a little while by covering the bowl, and leaving it over the hot water, after first adding a couple of spoons of cold water to the pan to lower the temperature and stop the cooking.

Serves 4.

This most delicious of sauces makes the perfect accompaniment for delicate green vegetables, such as asparagus, seakale, artichokes and broccoli.

MAYONNAISE

---

2 egg yolks
salt
½ teaspoon French mustard
or
a pinch dry mustard powder
1 cup olive oil
1–2 tablespoons white wine vinegar
or
fresh lemon juice

Bring all ingredients to room temperature. Break the yolks into a mortar or heavy bowl of generous size. Add a pinch of salt and the mustard. Beat thoroughly and steadily with a wooden spoon or the pestle (if using a mortar) for a few moments before starting to add the oil. While still beating steadily, start to add the oil drop by drop. Continue beating very slowly, until about 1/3 of the oil has been amalgamated, then start to add it more quickly. If the mayonnaise gets too thick to work easily, thin it down by adding a little of the vinegar—about 1 teaspoon, drop by drop. When all the oil is used, add more vinegar gradually to taste. Keep in a covered jar in the refrigerator till needed. If at any point the mayonnaise curdles, break another egg yolk into a clean bowl and add the curdled mayonnaise to it gradually, drop by drop, then add another ½ cup oil drop by drop. Mayonnaise is easier to make in large quantities; allow 1 egg yolk to ½ cup oil.

SAUCE REMOULADE

2 hard-boiled egg yolks
2 raw egg yolks
salt and black pepper
1 tablespoon Dijon mustard
2 tablespoons white wine vinegar
2 tablespoons tarragon vinegar
1 cup olive oil
6–8 tablespoons sour cream (optional)

Mash the hard-boiled egg yolks in a mortar, and beat in the raw egg yolks. Pound to a smooth creamy mixture, then add a pinch of salt and black pepper and the mustard. Continue to beat while you add the vinegar gradually, then the oil, drop by drop, as for mayonnaise. When you are finished, taste and adjust seasoning (it should taste quite strongly of mustard and vinegar). Beat in the sour cream if you want a lighter sauce, or omit.

Serves 4–6, but the quantities can easily be doubled.

SKORDALIA

4–5 large cloves garlic (about half a head)
1 large potato, boiled, peeled, and riced
2 slices stale white or brown bread, crusts removed
½ cup olive oil
1–2 tablespoons lemon juice
approximately 1 tablespoon milk

Peel the garlic and chop finely. Put in a mortar and pound until reduced to a mash. Add the potato and pound again until amalgamated. Soak the bread in water for 10 minutes. Squeeze the bread and add to the mixture. Pound the mixture again until reduced to a smooth pulp. Start to add the oil drop by drop, as you would for a mayonnaise, beating with the pestle or a wooden spoon. This sauce can separate as easily as a mayonnaise, so you must be very careful. If it shows signs of separating, beat in 1 tablespoon tepid water. Add lemon juice to taste, and beat in the milk to improve the color. It should be very pale, almost white.

Serves 4–6.

Good served with zucchini or eggplant fritters, hard-boiled eggs, boiled potatoes, fried fillets of fish.

ARABIAN SAUCE

4 ounces Philadelphia cream cheese
½ cup buttermilk
approximately 1 teaspoon lemon juice
½–1 teaspoon harissa
salt and black pepper

Cut the cheese in small pieces and put in the blender with the buttermilk. Stir in the lemon juice and the harissa, and add salt and black pepper. Heat for a hot sauce, or chill in the refrigerator.
　　Serves 4–6.

This very hot sauce is good with grilled chicken, couscous or grilled lamb kebabs. Harissa, a paste made from hot red peppers, is available in Eastern food shops.

CHEESE SOUFFLE SAUCE

4 tablespoons butter
3 tablespoons flour
1¼ cups milk
3 ounces grated Gruyère cheese
salt and black pepper
2 eggs, separated

Melt the butter, stir in the flour and cook for 3 minutes, stirring continuously. Heat the milk, add to the butter and flour mixture, and stir till smooth. Simmer for 5 minutes, stirring now and then, then add the grated cheese. Stir over gentle heat till smooth and melted. Season well with salt and black pepper. Beat the egg yolks lightly. Remove the mixture from the heat and beat in the egg yolks. Whip the whites and fold in. Pour over cooked vegetables and bake for 12 minutes at 400 degrees.
　　Serves 4–6.

This sauce is good with boiled asparagus, broccoli or leeks. It should be less solid than a soufflé, more like a foamy sauce.

CREAM CHEESE SAUCE

4 ounces Philadelphia cream cheese
½ cup buttermilk
1–2 teaspoons lemon juice
salt and black pepper

Dice the cheese and put in the blender with the buttermilk. Blend till smooth. Add lemon juice to taste. Season with salt and black pepper. Serve chilled, or heat gently without boiling.

Serves 4, but the recipe is easily doubled.

This is a good base for many cold sauces; it is quickly made and combines well with herbs, garlic or horseradish to make a good light, low-calorie dressing for cooked vegetable salads.

CREAM DRESSING

salt and black pepper
½ teaspoon sugar
1 tablespoon white wine vinegar
2 tablespoons thin cream
2 tablespoons olive oil

Put a pinch of salt, pepper and sugar in a small bowl. Pour in the vinegar and leave for a few moments to dissolve the seasonings. Add the cream and beat to blend. Pour in the oil and beat again.

Serves 6.

Excellent over lettuce salad or a mixture of cold cooked vegetables.

CREAM SAUCE

1 tablespoon butter
1 tablespoon flour
½ cup chicken stock
½ cup thin cream
3 tablespoons grated Gruyère cheese
salt and black pepper

Melt the butter, stir in the flour and cook for 3 minutes. Heat the stock and the cream together, pour into the *roux* and blend. Simmer for 4 minutes, then stir in the cheese until smooth. Season with salt and black pepper to taste.

   Serves 4.

This sauce is used as an accompaniment for egg dishes.

COLD CUCUMBER SAUCE

½ cucumber
1 tablespoon finely chopped onion
3 tablespoons sour cream
2 tablespoons mayonnaise (see p. 131)
Tabasco or anchovy essence to taste (about ½ teaspoon)
salt, black pepper and cayenne

Peel the cucumber and cut in small dice. Mix with the finely chopped onion. Beat the sour cream and the mayonnaise together and flavor to taste with Tabasco or anchovy essence. Season with salt and black pepper and a pinch of cayenne. Mix with the cucumber and onion and chill. Sprinkle with cayenne before serving.

   Serves 4.

Serve with grilled or fried sole.

DILL SAUCE

1½ tablespoons butter
1 tablespoon flour
½ cup stock: chicken, beef or veal
½ cup thin cream
salt and black pepper
3–4 tablespoons chopped dill
1 egg yolk (optional)

Melt the butter, stir in the flour and cook for 1 minute. Heat the stock and the cream together and pour into the *roux*. Stir until blended, and simmer for 4 minutes. Season with salt and black pepper and stir in the chopped dill. For a richer sauce beat the egg yolk in a cup and add a spoonful of the simmering sauce to it, then return to the pan and stir without boiling for 1 minute.

Serves 4—6.

Good with boiled beef.

GARLIC SAUCE WITH YOGHURT

1 large clove garlic
salt
½ cup yoghurt
herbs: 2 tablespoons chopped chives,
chervil, mint or dill

Mince the garlic, then pound it to a pulp in a mortar, adding a good pinch of salt. When reduced to a smooth paste add the yoghurt gradually, pounding after each addition to make a really smooth sauce. When all the yoghurt is amalgamated, add more salt to taste, and stir in the chopped herbs. Chill till ready to serve.

Serves 3—4.

Excellent with roast lamb, roast chicken, eggplant or zucchini fritters, grilled or fried eggplant and zucchini, grilled tomatoes, spinach soufflé or steamed broccoli mold.

HERB SAUCE

4 ounces Philadelphia cream cheese
½ cup buttermilk
about 1 tablespoon lemon juice
salt and black pepper
2—4 tablespoons mixed chopped herbs
(chervil, chives, dill, basil, tarragon)

Cut the cheese in pieces and put in the blender with the buttermilk. Blend till smooth. Add lemon juice, salt and black pepper to taste. Stir in the chopped herbs. The quantities should vary according to the strength of the herb: tarragon and basil are so strong that less is needed. Serve chilled or heat gently without allowing to boil.

Makes 1 cup.

Served over soft-boiled eggs, sliced cucumber or a mixed salad.

HORSERADISH SAUCE I

½ cup sour cream
3–4 tablespoons grated horseradish
1–2 teaspoons white wine vinegar
salt and black pepper

Stir the grated horseradish into the cream; add enough vinegar to flavor well. Season with salt and black pepper.

Makes ½ cup, serves 3–4.

Good with roast or boiled beef, smoked fish and beef stews.

HORSERADISH SAUCE II

½ cup mayonnaise made with lemon juice (see p. 131)
½ cup sour cream
4 tablespoons grated horseradish
lemon juice

Mix the mayonnaise and the sour cream together. Beat in the grated horseradish and add lemon juice to taste.

Makes 1¼ cups, serves 6.

This makes a creamier, richer sauce to serve with vegetable dishes like tomatoes.

COLD HORSERADISH SAUCE III

¼ pound Philadelphia cream cheese
½ cup buttermilk
approximately 1 tablespoon lemon juice
or
white wine vinegar
about 3 tablespoons grated horseradish
salt and black pepper

Cut the cheese in small pieces and put in the blender with the buttermilk. Blend till smooth, then pour into a bowl. Add 1 teaspoon lemon juice or vinegar, then stir in grated horseradish to taste. Add more lemon juice or vinegar, salt and black pepper to taste. Make several hours before needed to allow the flavor to develop. Chill in the refrigerator.

Makes a scant 1 cup, serves 4–6.

This is good poured over a dish of small peeled tomatoes, and is an excellent accompaniment to cold roast beef.

HORSERADISH AND APPLESAUCE

½ cup unsweetened applesauce
2 tablespoons horseradish, or more according to taste
2 tablespoons mayonnaise, made with lemon juice
(see p. 131)
2 tablespoons sour cream
lemon juice

Stir the horseradish into the applesauce. Stir in the mayonnaise and sour cream; add a little lemon juice to sharpen it. This sauce should be a perfect blending of the two flavors, so add enough horseradish to flavor it well without obscuring the taste of the apples.

Makes 1¼ cups, serves 6.

Excellent with cold duck, cold roast beef and cold pork.

HOT SAUCE

1 teaspoon ground cumin
1 teaspoon ground coriander
½ teaspoon chili powder
½ teaspoon celery salt
2 tablespoons tomato purée
2 tablespoons heated stock

Put the spices and tomato purée into a small bowl, pour on the hot stock and mix to a paste.

Serves 4.

A hot sauce to serve with couscous.

MINT SAUCE

3 tablespoons chopped fresh mint
or
1½ tablespoons dried mint
1 tablespoon sugar
3 tablespoons lemon juice
½ cup boiling water

Put the chopped mint in a mortar and pound. Add the sugar and pound again. Pour in the lemon juice, then the boiling water. Leave until cool.
Serves 2–4.

A traditional accompaniment to roast lamb.

SAUCE MORNAY I

2 cups milk
¼ bay leaf
½ small onion
2 cloves
6 black peppercorns
½ teaspoon salt
2 tablespoons butter
1½ tablespoons flour
3 ounces grated Gruyère cheese
½ cup cream

Put the milk in a small pan with the bay leaf, onion, cloves, peppercorns and salt. Bring to a boil, cover, set aside, and leave for 20 minutes to absorb the flavors. Melt the butter, stir in the flour and cook for 2 minutes, stirring constantly. Strain the milk mixture. Pour in the strained milk and blend. Simmer for 4 minutes, stirring often. Add the cheese by degrees, stirring over a very low heat until smooth. Add the cream and adjust seasoning to taste.
Serves 4–6.

This sauce is excellent poured over cooked vegetables, with some more grated cheese scattered over the top, and broiled for a few minutes.

SAUCE MORNAY II

3 teaspoons butter
1 tablespoon flour
½ cup chicken or vegetable stock or milk
½ cup thin cream
salt and pepper
3 ounces grated Gruyère cheese
1 egg yolk (optional)

Melt the butter, stir in the flour, and cook for 1 minute. Heat the stock or milk and cream in a small pan and pour into the *roux*. Blend and simmer for 4 minutes, stirring often. Stir in the grated cheese, and cook until melted and smooth. Season with salt and black pepper to taste. Add 1 egg yolk for a richer version.

Serves 4.

MUSHROOM SAUCE

¼ pound mushrooms
2 cups chicken stock
2 tablespoons butter
1½ tablespoons flour
¼ cup cream
salt and black pepper

Chop the mushrooms and cook in the stock for 20 minutes. Cool slightly, then put in the blender. Melt the butter in a clean pan, stir in the flour and blend. Cook for 2 minutes, then add the blended mushroom mixture. Simmer for 4 minutes, then add the cream and season to taste with salt and black pepper.

Serves 4.

Good with spinach pancakes; stuffed tomatoes.

MUSHROOM AND TOMATO SAUCE

6 ounces mushrooms
4 tablespoons butter
1 8-ounce can Italian peeled tomatoes

¼ teaspoon celery salt
¼ teaspoon sugar
2 tablespoons lemon juice
½ cup sour cream

Chop the mushrooms and toss in the butter until soft. Drain and cool. Put the tomatoes, mushrooms, seasonings, lemon juice and sour cream in a blender. Blend until smooth, taste and adjust seasoning if necessary. Pour into a small pan and simmer gently for 10 minutes.

Serves 8.

An excellent sauce for timbales, stuffed cabbage, soufflés.

ONION SAUCE

½ pound onions
2 cups chicken or beef stock
2 tablespoons butter
1½ tablespoons flour
salt and black pepper
¼ cup cream

Chop the onions coarsely and put in a pan with the stock. Bring to a boil, cover and simmer for 30 minutes. Cool slightly, then put in the blender. Melt the butter in a clean pan, stir in the flour and cook for 2 minutes. Pour on the blended onion mixture and simmer for 4 minutes. Add the cream, and season to taste with salt and freshly ground black pepper.

Serves 4.

Serve with boiled chicken or grilled lamb chops.

PISTOU OR PESTO

1½ cups fresh basil leaves
2 cloves garlic
4 tablespoons pine kernels (optional)
¾ cup grated Parmesan cheese
about 1 cup olive oil

Chop the basil and pound in a mortar. Add the chopped garlic and the chopped nuts. Pound all together, then add the cheese. Continue to pound until smooth and well blended, then beat in the oil, drop by drop, as for a mayonnaise. It should be the consistency of creamed butter.
    Serves 6.

An excellent sauce for gnocchi, spaghetti.

COLD SOUR CREAM SAUCE

½ cup sour cream
¼ cup canned vichysoisse
2 tablespoons catsup
2 shakes Tabasco
lemon juice (about ½ lemon)

Mix all the ingredients together, beat until smooth with an electric beater or whisk, and adjust seasoning to taste. Chill.
    Makes enough for 3–4.

An excellent sauce for salads of raw or cooked vegetables; also good with shellfish.

QUICK TOMATO SAUCE

½ pound tomatoes
½ cup sour cream
salt and black pepper

Skin the tomatoes and put them in the blender with the sour cream. Purée and add salt and black pepper to taste. For a hot sauce, heat gently without allowing to reach boiling point. For a cold sauce, serve as it is or chill in the refrigerator.
    Serves 4–6.

Good with stuffed vegetables, rice dishes, green timbales, molds or soufflés.

SPICY TOMATO SAUCE

4 ounces Philadelphia cream cheese
½ cup buttermilk
1–2 teaspoons lemon juice
salt and black pepper
1 tablespoon tomato purée
a few drops Tabasco or other chili sauce

Cut the cheese in small pieces and put in the blender with the buttermilk. Blend until smooth, then add lemon juice, salt and pepper, and tomato purée to taste and blend again. Add a few drops Tabasco and taste. When seasoning is correct, heat in a small pan without allowing to boil or chill in the refrigerator, depending on whether you want a hot or cold sauce.

Makes about 1 cup, serves 4–6.

Good as a cold sauce for shellfish, cucumber dishes or salads of white fish.

SMOOTH TOMATO SAUCE

1 14-ounce can tomatoes
2 tablespoons butter
2 tablespoons flour
½ cup chicken stock
½ cup thin cream
salt and black pepper

Drain the can of tomatoes and purée in a blender or put through the medium mesh of a vegetable mill. Melt the butter and stir in the flour. Heat the stock and pour in; stir till smooth and well blended. Add the tomato purée and bring to a boil. Simmer for 5 minutes, then add the cream and season to taste with salt and pepper.

THICK TOMATO SAUCE

1 small onion
2 tablespoons butter
¾ pound tomatoes
salt and black pepper
sugar

Melt the butter and cook the chopped onion till golden. Skin the tomatoes and chop coarsely. Add to the onion and cook gently for 8 minutes. Season with salt, black pepper and a pinch of sugar.

Serves 3—4.

This sauce can be served with a timbale of green peas.

SAUCE VINAIGRETTE I

salt and black pepper
3 tablespoons olive oil
1 tablespoon white wine vinegar

Put a pinch of salt and pepper from three or four turns of the peppermill in a small bowl and add the oil and vinegar. Beat well until mixed. This simplest form of *vinaigrette* is also known as French dressing.

Serves 4—6.

SAUCE VINAIGRETTE II

2 tablespoons finely chopped onion
2 tablespoons finely chopped parsley
1 tablespoon finely chopped chives, when available
salt and black pepper
1 clove garlic
½ teaspoon sugar
½ teaspoon mustard
2 tablespoons white wine vinegar
5 tablespoons olive oil

Put the chopped onion and herbs, a pinch of salt, pepper from about four turns of the peppermill, garlic, sugar and mustard in a bowl and add the vinegar slowly, beating with a wooden spoon. Add the oil gradually, beating until well mixed with the vinegar.

Serves 6.

This delicious sauce should be thick with onion and herbs; it is very good with boiled beef, either hot or cold. With the addition of a few chopped capers, it becomes the Italian *salsa verde*. Another good addition is one or two hard-boiled eggs, finely chopped.

SPINACH SAUCE

½ pound spinach
or
¼ pound package frozen chopped spinach
2 tablespoons butter
1 tablespoon flour
½ cup heated milk
½ cup thin cream
salt and black pepper
nutmeg

Cook the spinach, drain very well and chop. Melt the butter, stir in the flour, add the heated milk and the cream, stir until smooth and season well. Add a pinch of grated nutmeg. Stir in the chopped spinach. Put in the blender, then return to the cleaned pan to reheat. Taste for seasoning, and add a little extra milk if too thick.

Serves 6–8.

Serve over soft-boiled eggs; stuffed pancakes.

YOGHURT AND CREAM DRESSING

½ cup yoghurt
½ cup thin cream
½ teaspoon salt
black pepper
teaspoon sugar
4–6 tablespoons lemon juice

Beat the yoghurt and the cream together till blended. Add the seasonings and lemon juice to taste.

Serves 6.

A useful dressing for salads, as it is not too rich.

[12]

VEGETABLE ENCYCLOPEDIA

AGAR-AGAR

A gelatinous substance derived from various seaweeds; until recently this was eaten as food only in the Far East, while in Europe it has been used in chemical laboratories. It is now sold in health food shops as a substitute for gelatin. It has a natural gelatinous quality and, like all seaweeds, but unlike gelatin, is full of iron and other minerals. Agar-agar has no taste of its own, so can be put to any purpose. In the East it is used by swallows for building their nests, thus is one of the ingredients of birds' nest soup.

ARTICHOKE

This succulent vegetable is the flower of a decorative thistle. Although a native of North Africa, it grows happily in Europe and North America. In Europe artichokes are in season throughout the summer; in America practically all the year round. There are numerous varieties, some producing flat round heads with smooth-edged leaves, like the Brittany artichoke; others with more pointed heads and leaves, like the Paris artichoke.

In many recipes only the delicate *fond d'artichaut* is called for. The term refers to the bottom of the artichoke, while *coeur d'artichaut* means the bottom with the innermost tender leaves still adhering to it, the choke having been removed. The bottoms alone can be used for a number of elegant dishes such as soufflés, bases for purées of chopped vegetables, *eggs Sardou*, scrambled eggs with chopped truffles, as part of the French dish *filets de sole Murat*, as garnishes, or as one of the ingredients of a salad.

Whole artichokes are always served at the start of a meal, either hot, with melted butter, or cold, with a *sauce vinaigrette* or mayonnaise. Rich in iron and other minerals, they are very sustaining and the large ones practically make a meal in themselves.

To prepare: Trim the stalks of the artichoke, remove any discolored outer leaves, wash well under running water, and soak for 15 minutes in cold water. Drain upside down in a colander before cooking. Some people trim off the sharp ends of the leaves with scissors; this has the advantage of reducing them in size if you do not have a large enough pot in which to cook them, otherwise it is not worth the trouble.

There are two ways to prepare artichoke bottoms. One way is to cook the whole artichoke first, then discard the leaves and choke when they are cool enough to handle. Some people prefer to cut off all the leaves and most of the stem before cooking, leaving only the choke to be removed after the artichoke is cooked.

To cook either whole artichokes or the bottoms alone, bring a very large pan of salted water to a boil and throw in the drained artichokes. Bring back to a boil and cook briskly for 35—50 minutes, according to size. Test to see if they are cooked by pulling away one of the outer leaves; if it comes away from the head without undue pressure, they are ready. If still in doubt test by piercing the center of the base with a fork. As soon as they are cooked, lift them out and drain upside down in a colander. When cooking the bottoms alone, the timing will probably be about 30–35 minutes; test with a fork.

Hot artichokes should be served on a flat dish with the sauce in a separate bowl. They look elegant wrapped in a white linen napkin. The choke is sometimes removed with a narrow spoon and some of the sauce poured into the center of the artichoke.

Cold artichokes are at their best about one hour after cooking. If you are using only the bottoms, sprinkle them with lemon juice to prevent discoloring.

ASPARAGUS

Asparagus has been esteemed as one of the greatest delicacies of the table since Roman times. There are a great many different varieties, each prized in its own country. The French and Belgians like the thick white stalks ending in pale purple tips, known as *argenteuil*, while in the United States and England, the thinner green variety, closer to the wild one, is preferred. Both are excellent in their own ways. Asparagus comes into season in June and July.

It is rich in minerals and vitamins, and should be cooked in the minimum of water or in a steamer in order to preserve them as well as the flavor.

To prepare: Trim the asparagus stalks to an equal length, wash the green tips under running water, and using a sharp knife, scrape the woody white part of the stem. Then tie the asparagus in bundles with fine string, leaving long ends with which to lower them in and out of the water. Ideally asparagus should be cooked upright, with water coming halfway up the stems. Special pans are made for this purpose, but an alternative method can be devised using a double boiler, with the top half inverted over the bottom, so that only the stems are in water, while the tender tips cook more gently in the steam. Failing this they can be cooked horizontally in a rectangular pan with a strainer which makes it easier to lift them out of the water without breaking any of the tips.

They should be cooked in already boiling, lightly salted water for about 10–30 minutes, depending on the thickness. The best way to test them for doneness is to hold one stalk upright; the tip should start to bend over about two thirds of the way up. Alternatively pierce the stalk halfway up with a skewer. Do not expect the very bottom of the stalk to become soft. Lift them out of the water and drain well. Asparagus is served either hot or cold with the main course, and the tips are also used as a garnish for many dishes. When at its best, asparagus should be served as simply as possible, that is to say, well drained, laid on a flat dish or wrapped in a white linen napkin, with a jug of melted butter handed separately and a bowl of salt. For a more elaborate dish it can be served with a *sauce hollandaise* or a *sauce maltaise*. In Belgium it is often served with melted butter and a plate of halved hard-boiled eggs; each person takes half an egg and mashes the yolk into some of the melted butter on his plate, which gives a delicious, slightly thicker sauce. They are also good served cold, with a *sauce vinaigrette*, or covered with a *sauce mornay* and browned under the broiler. Another good dish is to beat a couple of egg whites into the *sauce mornay* and put the dish in a hot oven until the sauce has risen slightly and set like a soufflé. When the tips alone are used as garnishes the English green variety is the best.

Although, strictly speaking, this plant is the fruit of the avocado tree, it is usually treated as a vegetable. A native of South America, it has flesh of a soft texture and a subtle flavor. Avocado is full of vitamins and minerals, an extremely nourishing food, although it is rather high in calories. The fruits should be chosen with care by applying the lightest pressure to test for a slight softness. They should not be bruised or have black marks. Like most fruit, avocado can be bought while still unripe and allowed to ripen at a sunny window.

To prepare: Avocado is generally eaten raw. It is quite delicious when eaten alone or in a green salad. It is best when served with something that has a sharp taste for contrast to the blandness of the avocado. Cut the avocado in half, remove the stone and sprinkle with lemon to prevent discoloring if the avocado is not to be used immediately.

AVOCADO

A native of Japan, this tiny hard red bean is grown extensively throughout China and Japan. In the East the beans are cooked in both their fresh and dried states, but in the United States, they are usually found dried in health food or Oriental shops.

To prepare: Dried azuki beans take an extremely long time to cook, and should be soaked beforehand for several hours or overnight. After soaking they must be cooked about 2 hours to become soft.

AZUKI BEANS

Batavia is a variety of endive. The shape and the color are similar, with pale yellow leaves in the center surrounded by darker green leaves,

BATAVIA

but the leaves are broader and rounder in shape, and less curly. It is in season at the same time as chicory, and has a similar though less bitter taste.

To prepare: Batavia can be treated in exactly the same way as chicory and eaten either raw, as is most often done, or cooked.

BAMBOO SHOOTS

These are the tender young shoots of the bamboo cane. A native of Malay, it can be grown in temperate parts of England and the United States. The shoots form one of the main ingredients of Chinese cooking, where they are used in their fresh state, but they are also canned and sold extensively throughout the United States.

To prepare: Bamboo shoots can be sautéed or steamed like any other tender vegetable such as asparagus or seakale, or eaten raw in salads.

BEAN SPROUTS

These are the young shoots of a variety of soybean, and are used extensively in Chinese cookery. They can be bought in cans or packages, or they can easily be grown at home after the fashion of mustard.

To prepare: Bean sprouts can be steamed in a matter of 4–5 minutes over boiling stock or water, or simmered for 4–5 minutes in liquid. Alternatively they can be sautéed in a very little hot oil for 5 minutes, stirred now and then.

BEAN CURD

Bean curd is made from the soybean, and has the same high vitamin content. It is extremely cheap and nourishing, and forms one of the basic foods for the Chinese. It can be bought in Chinese food shops, is easy to cook and very versatile. It combines well with most other foods—fish, meat or other vegetables.

To prepare: Bean curd is usually deep-fried. It should be cut in cubes about 1-inch square, dropped into hot oil and fried until crisp and golden brown on the outside and soft on the inside. It can also be boiled.

A native of Southern Europe, the beet plays an important part in the cuisine of Poland and Russia. There are an amazing number of different varieties: one reference book illustrates eighteen totally different plants, ranging in shape and size from a giant carrot-shaped root to a flat squat object like a tiny turnip. In the United States, people favor the round variety with dark red flesh. Beets are sold fresh or canned, already prepared.

BEET

To prepare: Twist off the leaves carefully (if young and fresh, they can be cooked separately and served as a green vegetable; they are even richer in vitamins than the roots). Scrub the beet gently under a running tap to remove all the dirt, being careful not to puncture the skin. Buy small ones whenever possible. Large ones take longer to cook and one cannot cut beets in pieces without losing the color except by cutting them in pieces and cooking in a minimum of water, so that it has all evaporated by the end of the cooking and the color remains in the beet. This is quite tricky, however, as they still take a considerable time to cook, and the water has to be replenished to prevent its boiling away entirely. To cook in the normal fashion, put in a large pan covered with cold water, add salt, and bring to a boil. Cook until soft when pierced with a fork—at this stage they will not bleed. Allow up to 2 hours for small roots. They can also be baked in the oven like potatoes, taking 1½—2 hours. After cooking, beets can be cut in thick slices or chunks and tossed in melted butter or thick cream. Serve these with a handful of chopped fresh herbs—dill is particularly good with beets. Season well with salt and black pepper. Already cooked beets can be cut in slices or coarsely grated and reheated in a pan with cream and herbs, or butter or sour cream, and plenty of salt and black pepper. Be careful that they do not stick to the pan as they have a high sugar content and burn easily. Beets make excellent soups, not only the well-known borscht, a classic soup of Russia, but also delicate summer consommes, to serve hot, chilled, or jellied.

BELGIUM ENDIVE

Belgium, also sometimes called French, endive is a long thin vegetable with overlapping white leaves edged with pale green, and a curious slightly bitter taste. It is a native of Europe, and has been used for hundreds of years in salads and medicines. The cultivated variety is blanched to achieve the desired white leaf, and the bitterness is greatly reduced. It is in season from November to March.

To prepare: Endive is generally used raw as part of a mixed salad, either with the leaves left whole or torn into pieces, or the whole plant cut across in thick slices. It also combines well with beets. If cooked, it should be placed whole in a heavy casserole, arranged in layers with a little stock or water, a generous piece of butter, a little lemon juice and a pinch of salt. Cover and cook in the oven for 45 minutes. Belgium endive also makes a delicious filling for a pastry quiche, or can be served braised and covered with a good cheese sauce.

BROCCOLI

Broccoli is a form of cauliflower and is in season during the winter and early spring. It is rich in vitamin C, and has a more delicate flavor than the cauliflower. There are two main types of broccoli: The green sprouting one is also known by its Italian name *calabrese*, while the purple sprouting variety is sometimes called "asparagus broccoli." There is also a large-headed variety with a compact flower, like a small cauliflower except in color, the flower being usually purple or green, although there are also white varieties.

To prepare: Sprouting broccoli, the most common form, is not easy to cook to perfection, as the tough stalks take far longer to cook than the delicate head. The best method is to cook it in two stages: chop the stalks and put them in a fairly broad pan containing just enough lightly salted boiling water to cover them, replace the lid and cook for 5 minutes. Then lay the flower heads whole on the top and leave them to cook in the steam. After another 6–7 minutes, both parts of the vegetable should be tender; if the heads are ready first, they can be lifted out carefully and kept warm while the stalks finish cooking. They should then be drained and arranged round the edges of the serving dish with the flower heads in the middle. Melted butter seasoned with salt and black pepper should then be poured over all. Broccoli can also be steamed, by cooking the stalks for 6–8 minutes before adding the heads, which are cooked for another 6–8 minutes.

The large-headed broccoli is much easier to cook, and should be treated like a small cauliflower. Leave it whole, just trimming off the end of the stalk and the outer leaves, and choose a pan that fits it neatly. Measure enough water to come halfway up the broccoli, then remove it while you bring the salted water to a boil. Put the broccoli in stalk downwards, cover the pan and cook until the stalk is just tender. Drain carefully and lay in a round serving dish. Melt some butter with salt and black pepper and pour over it, or pass a *sauce hollandaise* in a separate bowl. Broccoli has a special affinity with eggs and butter, and is delicious served with sauces made of these foods, or with scrambled eggs.

BRUSSELS SPROUTS

This ungainly member of the cabbage family is not a decorative plant, unlike most varieties of cabbage, but is an extremely useful winter vegetable, in season from October till March. It was first developed in Belgium, as the name suggests. It is rich in vitamins B and C, and has a good nutty flavor. The sprouts are borne along the length of the stems, which grow to a height of 1½–2 feet. Unlike most other members of the same family, it does not form a head, but only a loose rosette of leaves at the top of the stem.

To prepare: Very small sprouts need little or no preparation beyond washing; the slightly larger ones should have the stem trimmed and cut with an X-shaped cross, so that the stalk will cook more quickly. Bring a large pan of salted water to a boil, and throw in the sprouts. Bring back to a boil as quickly as possible and cook briskly until tender, about 10 minutes. Drain well, and return to the pan to dry out over gentle heat. When all excess moisture has evaporated, add a generous lump of butter and grind plenty of salt and black pepper over them. Brussels sprouts are excellent if after draining they are quickly chopped with a long knife, returned to the pan and tossed in melting butter and salt and black pepper. They go particularly well with dishes of roast or grilled lamb.

CABBAGE

The name "cabbage" covers an enormous family of plants that have been cultivated throughout Europe and western Asia since the earliest records. They were used by the Romans, as much for their supposed medicinal qualities as for their nourishment. The family includes cauliflower, celery, broccoli, kale, Brussels sprouts, and kohlrabi, all listed separately. See *also* green cabbage, white cabbage, and red cabbage.

CARDOON

Like the globe artichoke, the cardoon is a member of the thistle family, and is a native of Southern Europe. It was popular in England some two hundred years ago but is now rarely seen, although it is still much prized in Europe and quite common in the United States. The plants grow to an even larger size than the artichoke, and resemble a giant form of celery. Like celery, both the stalks and the roots are edible.

To prepare: Cut the stalks into pieces of equal length and scrape off the outer skin, sprinkling lemon juice to prevent discoloration. Cut off the outer covering of the root and rub lemon juice over it. The cardoon is best cooked like celery, only allow much more time. The stalks should be braised or stewed slowly in stock or salted water. They may take 1½–2 hours to become tender. Some of the stock can then be used to make a sauce, seasoned with chopped parsley. Cardoons are also good served with a well-flavored cream sauce, or a *sauce mornay*. They may be made into a purée by pushing through a sieve or vegetable mill, and mixing with an equal quantity of potato purée. Beat in some butter, a little cream, and season well with salt and black pepper.

CARRAGEEN

Also known as Irish moss, this seaweed grows on the coasts of the British Isles, and parts of North America. Like all edible seaweeds, it is extremely rich in minerals, especially iodine. It has strong gelatinous qualities, and a commercially prepared form is sold in health food shops as a "vegetable gelatin."

To prepare: The dried seaweed should be soaked for at least 30 minutes, then put in a pan with three times its own bulk of water or milk. Simmer gently for 30 minutes, stirring occasionally. A pinch of salt should be added during the cooking, and a flavoring such as lemon rind, ginger, or vanilla, if desired. After the cooking it should be strained to get rid of any pieces that have not dissolved, then it should be allowed to set until it jells. Sugar can be added to taste, while a beaten egg white or whipped cream can be folded in before it has set.

CARROTS

A native of Europe, the wild carrot must have been growing for hundreds of years before the first cultivated variety was introduced during the seventeenth century. Carrots are in season year-round, but the most delicious are the new carrots in the early summer. There are many different varieties of carrot, ranging from long thin tapering roots to short stumpy turnip-shaped ones. The color also varies from a pale yellow to a dark reddish orange. The most popular in the United States is a medium-length orange root.

Carrots are immensely rich in vitamin A, and possess quantities of vitamin C and minerals. All these precious nutrients are stored close to the surface of the root, which must be treated with care to conserve them. New carrots need only a light brushing under running water, while older ones should be scraped with a sharp knife, being careful to remove only the minimum of skin.

To prepare: When new, carrots are best cooked whole, in which case they should be covered with cold lightly salted water, brought to a boil, and cooked until tender, about 15—20 minutes. Drain and return to the pan with a pat of butter, a sprinkling of sugar, and serve with chopped parsley sprinkled over them. Older and larger carrots are best cut in thin slices. These pieces should be put in a pan with a very little cold water, just enough to cover the bottom of the pan, and a pinch of salt and sugar. Bring to a boil, cover the pan and cook gently for about 15 minutes, shaking the pan from time to time. Check now and then to see that all the water has not boiled away. After 10 minutes put in a pat of butter; after another 5 minutes the carrots should be tender or nearly so, while the cooking liquid should have reduced to a couple of spoonfuls of buttery juice. If there is still too much liquid, remove the carrots with a slotted spoon, and reduce by fast boiling till slightly thickened and syrupy. Taste to make sure it does not get too salty. Serve the carrots in their juice.

Raw carrots are richer in vitamins than cooked ones; they can either be made into a delicious juice with a juice extractor, or grated and served as a salad, either alone or mixed with other grated raw vegetables such as celery, white cabbage, hard fruits like apples, and chopped nuts. The juice also can be drunk alone, or mixed with others such as spinach, watercress, or tomato. Carrots are also one of the more valuable flavoring vegetables for stocks and stews, while a sliced carrot is almost always included in a court bouillon for poaching fish. They make excellent soups and purées, either alone, or mixed with other root vegetables.

CAULIFLOWER

The cauliflower, a member of the cabbage family, has been developed for the sake of its flower, a compact white head surrounded by tender pale green leaves, with a delicate flavor which requires careful treatment in the kitchen.

To prepare: There are a choice of methods of cooking the cauliflower; the plant can be left whole, which looks pretty, or it can be divided into sprigs, which facilitates the cooking. If left whole, the stalk should be cut with a deep X, to hasten the cooking of the toughest part. Choose a pan just large enough to contain it, and measure enough water to come halfway up the vegetable. Remove the cauliflower while you bring the salted water to a boil, then put it in and cover the pan. Cook briskly for about 10 minutes, then start testing it with a fork every two minutes, and remove it as soon as the stalk is reasonably tender. It must never be allowed to cook for a moment longer than is necessary to become tender, as it very quickly turns into a watery mass of an unappetizing pallor. It should be removed from the cooking water while it is still definitely crisp and firm, drained well in a colander and dressed with melting butter. A careful seasoning with salt and black pepper is essential; an additional garnish of chopped hard-boiled egg, parsley and/or browned bread crumbs can be added if desired. A good cheese sauce is made with some of the cooking water reduced and mixed in equal quantities with thin cream, and flavored with grated cheese, usually Parmesan. If you put flavor above appearance, it is probably better to divide the cauliflower into sprigs before cooking. This is certainly a simpler method as the pieces are all roughly equal in size, and are cooked at the same time. Bring just enough lightly salted water to cover the washed sprigs to a boil, throw them in, and cook for 8—10 minutes, removing from the fire as soon as they are beginning to soften. Drain well, tip them into a shallow dish, and serve with melted butter seasoned with salt and black pepper, and possibly a cream sauce, or a cheese sauce.

Cauliflower also makes a delicious cold dish, the cooked sprigs mixed with quartered hard-boiled eggs and dressed with a *sauce vinaigrette* flavored with finely chopped fresh herbs. A thin mayonnaise can replace the vinaigrette, and the eggs can be omitted. To be at its best, the cauliflower should be only just cooked, and dressed immediately with the sauce, then allowed to cool just before eating. It is much better to eat it while still slightly warm than completely cold. It is also delicious eaten raw, and extremely healthy, as it is full of vitamins A, B, and C and mineral salts. To eat raw, it should be finely chopped or grated; the stalks can be finely chopped and the flowers grated over the top.

CELERIAC or CELERY ROOT

Celeriac is an extremely useful winter vegetable. Not only does it contain more iron than almost any other food, it has the flavor of celery without its stringy texture, which makes it better suited for cooking. The swollen root is irregularly shaped, and can be eaten raw or cooked. The classic French hors-d'oeuvre, *celeri remoulade*, is made with raw shredded celeriac mixed with a well-seasoned *sauce remoulade*. It can also be grated or shredded and sprinkled over a salad but it must first be pared quite thickly.

To prepare: Peeled celeriac should be cut in slices or chunky pieces and covered with cold salted water. Bring to a boil and simmer until soft, about 30 minutes, depending on the size of the pieces. Drain well, and make into a purée with an equal quantity of freshly boiled potatoes. Beat in a little butter or cream, season carefully with salt and black pepper, and serve. A thinner version, cooked in stock instead of water, then puréed with the stock, makes an excellent and very nourishing soup. Celeriac needs a sprinkling of chopped parsley for contrast. The flavor goes particularly well with all sorts of game. Slices of celeriac, parboiled, can be made into fritters by dipping in batter and deep-frying.

CELERY

A native of Great Britain, celery can be found growing wild in fields and marshes. The cultivated variety is quite hard to grow. It contains valuable quantities of minerals, and vitamin C, but not as much iron as celeriac. Its ridged, concave stalks have a delicious crisp texture and cleansing taste when eaten raw.

To prepare: The best method of cooking celery is to braise it. It is often used as part of a mixed raw vegetable salad, chopped in small pieces. The pale leaves are also good, and should be chopped and used as a garnish or mixed with salad. A dish of braised celery is the classic accompaniment to roast pheasant; it is also indispensable for flavoring soups, stews and stocks. A celery stalk forms part of a *bouquet garni:* the other ingredients, bay leaf, two or three stalks of parsley, and thyme, are wrapped in the hollow of the celery stalk and tied with thread.

CHICKPEAS

These rocklike objects are much used in the Middle East, Spain, Morocco and parts of France and Italy. Like all dried vegetables they are rich in vitamins, but they take an extremely long time to cook. They have a curious flavor which is not liked by all, but once one has acquired a taste for them, as in the Arab dish *homus* made with sesame seed paste, one can't live for long without them. They are also one of the ingredients of the classic couscous, and are made into nourishing soups and stews, or eaten cold as garnish for salads.

To prepare: Chickpeas should be soaked overnight, then brought very slowly to a boil in a large pan. Simmer gently for one hour, adding flavoring vegetables. Then add salt, and cook for another hour, or until soft. If for a cold dish, they should be drained and dressed with olive oil while still hot. As they take so long to cook, it is sensible to cook enough for two dishes at one time. Half the peas can be kept in their cooking liquid until the following day, then made into an excellent soup.

CHINESE CABBAGE

This unusual vegetable is really more like a lettuce than a cabbage, and can be used in place of either. Chinese cabbage is available year-round.

To prepare: The crisp leaves can be shredded and eaten raw, as in cole slaw, or cooked quickly in the minimum of boiling salted water for only a few minutes, and drained well. They can also be steamed or sautéed, as they are generally treated in Chinese restaurants. The leaves are also suited to stuffing, being a more convenient shape than the round cabbage, and of a stronger consistency than the lettuce.

COLLARDS

Collards is a general term which covers all sorts of greens that do not form a head, such as kale, turnip tops, and chard. They were frequently mentioned in medieval English cookery books, and they are still a familiar term in soul food cookery. Collards are a good source of vitamins during the winter months.

CORN-ON-THE-COB

See SWEET CORN.

CUCUMBER

A native of Asia and Egypt, the cucumber was not introduced to the West until the late sixteenth century. Part of a large family which includes squash, gourds and melons, the cucumber is borne on a creeping plant with herbaceous stems. Although there are many different varieties, such as the white or yellow cucumber, and a range of sizes and shapes, the most popular in the United States is the familiar long straight fruit, with pale green flesh enclosed in dark green smooth or slightly ridged skin. There are also special varieties grown specially for pickling that are smaller than the normal cucumber.

Full of vitamins B and C, the cucumber has no fat content or carbohydrate, which makes it ideal for dieters. It has a cool refreshing quality that makes it delicious for summer meals, or as an accompaniment to curries and other hot dishes.

To prepare: Some people slice and salt cucumber for some time before eating in order to make it limp and more easily digested. Others like to keep its crisp texture and don't bother to salt it in advance. The cucumber may be peeled or unpeeled according to personal preference.

Cucumber can be cooked in the manner of a zucchini; although usually eaten raw, it is delicious hot, and very quick and easy to prepare. It can be left unpeeled, cut in thick slices (about ¼ inch), and gently fried on each side in butter. To serve, sprinkle with chopped chervil or dill. It can also be cut in very thin slices and coated in flour or dipped in batter and fried in deep fat. It can be cut in oval shapes, or small balls, and tossed in butter as a garnish for a sole or trout or a fillet of veal. It makes a pretty aspic ring, either alone or mixed with diced tomato, or a variety of excellent sauces—hot, cold or semi-frozen—to accompany fish or vegetable dishes.

DANDELION GREENS

The dandelion is a weed that grows all over Europe and North America. In France and Italy the young leaves that appear in the spring are much prized as a salad vegetable and cultivated as such, but in England and the United States, it only grows wild. It is rich in iron and minerals and in vitamins A and C. It is believed by many to have medicinal qualities and is worth searching for, in any case, because of its refreshing sharp taste.

To prepare: Use only the very young leaves. Dandelion greens are much improved by being blanched, which can be done by covering the plant with an inverted flower pot for ten days before using. The leaves lose some of their bitterness when treated in this way, and are more easily digested.

The leaves can be eaten raw as a salad, either alone or with other salad vegetables, or they can be cooked like spinach. They make an excellent salad mixed with diced bacon fried crisp.

EGGPLANT

Although the eggplant is connected with Mediterranean cookery, it is a native of India and other parts of Asia. It is a fruit of rare beauty, purple in color and varying in shape from round to oval and globular forms. There is also a white variety, which must have given rise to its name, as it is curiously like the egg of some gigantic exotic bird, with its translucent glow. It is more often used for decorative purposes than for cooking. Eggplants are almost always available.

To prepare: The stalks should be removed with a sharp knife, and the eggplants washed or wiped with a damp cloth. According to how they are to be cooked, they are then cut in halves or quarters, sliced or chopped, usually with the peel left on. They are then sprinkled with salt and left to drain for about half an hour; this gets rid of the slightly bitter taste they sometimes have. If possible choose fairly young ones, before the seeds have had time to form. Before cooking rinse off the salt and pat dry in a cloth or soft paper.

Eggplants can be cooked whole, baked in the oven like potatoes. They will take about 45 minutes at a moderate temperature (350 degrees), and can be tested with a skewer. This is usually done when only the inner pulp is wanted for a purée. They can also be boiled, whole or cut in half, or broiled. Eggplants are often cut in slices, unpeeled and fried in oil. They have to be done in batches, a few at a time, as they must all be in one layer, so they take some time to do, and consume huge quantities of oil. After cooking drain them on soft paper and keep in a warm place till needed. Eggplants are one of the main ingredients of *ratatouille*, a dish in which they are stewed in oil with tomatoes, onions, peppers and zucchini, and also make a delicious gratin mixed with sliced tomatoes and cooked in the oven. They are an extremely versatile vegetable and can be used for stuffing, as is often done in Greece, and they can be eaten equally well hot or cold, stuffed with mixtures of meat and rice, or rice and pine nuts.

ENDIVE

A native of the East, endive was brought to the West in the sixteenth century, where it was highly thought of as a salad vegetable. It is a green vegetable, rather like a round lettuce in shape, with very curly leaves, pale yellow in the center and darker green around the edges. Only the pale leaves should be used, as the green parts are bitter. It is extremely rich in vitamins B and C and minerals, including iron. As it is in season during the winter, it makes a good substitute for lettuce.

To prepare: Endive is delicious mixed with watercress and Belgium endive. When it is eaten raw, only the pale leaves should be used.

The leaves can also be cooked, in which case the darker ones are also used. Cook for 12 minutes in lightly salted boiling water and drain very well. Chop the leaves and return to the pan. Mix with a good cream sauce, season carefully and serve.

ESCAROLE

See BATAVIA.

FENNEL

Fennel has a bulbous root base and a strange taste somewhat like celery with overtones of anise.

To prepare: When young and tender, the roots can be thinly sliced and eaten raw, dressed with olive oil and lemon juice, either alone or mixed with tomatoes, radishes, or other salad vegetables. When cooked it is best cut in half and braised in the manner of celery. It can be cooked either on top of the stove or in the oven. Dot the fennel with butter, sprinkle with a little lemon juice and chicken or vegetable stock, then cook gently, turning over now and then, for about 1½ hours.

FLAGEOLETS

See HARICOT BEANS.

GARLIC

A relative of the onion, garlic is a bulbous root which is a native of Southern Europe. It can easily be grown by the amateur; the outer cloves should be separated and planted in a sunny position in well-drained soil. Garlic has a very strong flavor. When eaten raw, as in salads or *aioli*, the French garlic mayonnaise, its taste is exceptionally strong; in long cooking it becomes milder.

To prepare: Rarely is more than one clove used in a recipe. Separate the clove and peel. If the clove will not be removed from the food at the end of cooking, it should be finely minced.

GOURDS

An enormous family of vegetables, the gourds include popular cooking varieties such as pumpkins, squash, zucchini, cucumbers and melons, and the decorative varieties, also edible, but used mainly for decorative purposes. The decorative gourds come in all shapes, colors and sizes, and after picking they can be dried and kept as decoration for winter, when flowers are scarce. The edible gourds are listed separately under their individual names.

GREEN BEANS

Also known as string beans or snap beans, these are grown for their pods rather than their seeds. They originated in South America, and did not appear in Europe until the sixteenth century. They are quite high in mineral content and in vitamin B; when the beans are dried, they become an even richer source of vitamins.

To prepare: Tender young string beans are usually best left whole. Nip off the ends just before tossing them into boiling water, just enough to cover, and cooking them for a short time, 10–15 minutes. They should be quickly drained and tossed lightly in butter. Green beans can also be steamed. When served hot, they may be garnished with chopped onion or bacon; when served cold, they are good dressed with a *sauce vinaigrette.*

GREEN CABBAGE

This is the best-known cabbage in the United States. It is rich in vitamins C, E and K, and in mineral salts which are all too often lost in the cooking. There are two main subdivisions of green cabbage: the smooth-leaved, and the curly-leaved or Savoy, cabbage. The former is the more widely grown, but the Savoy is generally considered to have a more delicate flavor.

To prepare: Both types of green cabbage should be treated in the same way. Remove the leaves from the stem and wash carefully. Only the tender inner leaves should be used in most cases, but if the tougher ones are to be included the stems should be cut in a V-shape at their largest part (the base of the leaf). The leaves can then be left whole, torn into pieces 4 or 5 inches across, or chopped. Put a couple of inches of lightly salted water in a large pan and bring to a boil. When it bubbles, add the drained cabbage and cover the pan. Cook fairly rapidly, turning over the cabbage from time to time, and making sure the water does not boil away. As soon as the stems are tender but still crisp when pierced, drain thoroughly. Return to the pan and set on low heat, stirring constantly to evaporate as much moisture as possible. When the cabbage is more or less dry, add a good lump of butter and plenty of salt and black pepper. Alternatively turn out onto a board and chop, returning to the pan with butter and seasoning. Green cabbage can also be made into a purée by pushing through the coarse mesh of a vegetable mill; when using a blender, it has a tendency to become watery. Cabbage can also be simmered very gently in milk. Reserve the milk and thicken with a beaten egg yolk, season the sauce with salt and black pepper, and pour it back over the cabbage. Surrounded with croutons of toast or bread fried in butter, this makes an excellent dish. For a more substantial dish such as is often seen in Central European cuisine, a whole cabbage or individual leaves can be stuffed with a variety of different fillings. This makes a pretty and sustaining main course for a vegetable meal, especially when served with a contrasting sauce.

HARICOT BEANS

Although these are usually thought of in their dried state, they can also be eaten fresh, as they are in France and Italy, and are quite delicious.

Dried haricot beans are extremely useful as a source of vitamins during the winter; for some reason, they gain in nutritional value through the drying process. The quality of dried vegetables depends greatly on their age and the length of time they have been in store. It is well worth stocking up from a reliable foreign foods shop in the autumn, when the fresh crops come in. They are also cheap and filling food for cold weather. They make an excellent soup (see p. 5), and are a delicious accompaniment to roast lamb.

To prepare: Wash the dried beans well in a colander, throwing away any wrinkled or discolored beans, then put them in a large pan well-covered with cold, unsalted water. Bring it slowly to a boil, then cover the pan and turn off the heat. After one hour they are ready for the final cooking, either in the same liquid, with an onion, a carrot, a stalk of celery, a bay leaf and a few stalks of parsley, or in stock. Bring them back to a boil and simmer gently until they are tender; another hour's cooking should be enough unless they are old. Do not add salt until they are nearly done as it makes them tough. Fresh haricot beans are cooked in the same way as lima beans.

HEARTS OF PALM

These delicacies, the tender young shoots of a variety of palm tree, can be bought canned. They make an excellent hors-d'oeuvre and are delicious in green salads.

To prepare: Simply drain the hearts and cover with a good *sauce vinaigrette*.

HORSERADISH

As the classic accompaniment to roast beef, horseradish has been grown in England since the sixteenth century. It was brought to the United States from England. Most people today seem to prefer the ready-made sauce or bottled grated horseradish.

To prepare: The root needs to be well scrubbed under running water, then scraped or grated. It can be piled in little mounds on slices of rare beef, or it can be made into excellent sauce by mixing with cream and lemon juice or adding it to a mayonnaise. (For recipes, see pp. 137–138.)

The Jerusalem artichoke is a native of North America, where it is particularly popular in Pennsylvania Dutch kitchens. Its name has remained something of a mystery: "Artichoke" is taken to refer to the slight similarity in flavor between this root and the bottom of the globe artichoke, while "Jerusalem" is believed to be a corruption of the Italian word for sunflower, *girasola*. The misshapen tuberous growths on the roots, similar in appearance to a potato, are the edible part of this plant. Jerusalem artichokes are very nourishing and rich in carbohydrates.

To prepare: Jerusalem artichokes are extremely difficult to clean, some varieties being even more uneven and knobby than others. The best method is to scrub them carefully before cooking and to peel them afterwards. Cover lightly with cold water and boil until tender, about 15 minutes. Drain them and peel as soon as they are cool enough to handle. They make an excellent puree, either alone or mixed with an equal part of mashed potatoes or other root vegetables. They can also be made into an excellent soup, in which case you should reserve their cooking liquid for stock. They are delicious as a first course, cut into slices and covered with butter and chopped parsley, *sauce mornay* or *sauce hollandaise*.

JERUSALEM ARTICHOKES

KALE

Also known as borecole, Scotch kale, curly kail, colewort, and in the South as collards, kale is the earliest form of cabbage. It is a beautiful vegetable, with tightly curled leaves of a dark bluish-green, which do not form a heart. They are full of vitamins.

To prepare: Bring a large pan of lightly salted water to a boil, throw in the leaves, either whole or torn in pieces, and boil rapidly till tender. Drain very well, chop on a flat board with a long knife, return to the pan and reheat with a lump of butter and plenty of salt and black pepper. In Scotland it is traditionally cooked with oatmeal in a dish called *kail brose,* a sort of thick soup. It is also good boiled and served with egg sauce, or it can be made into a purée mixed with equal parts of potato, and with hot milk, butter and seasonings added.

KOHLRABI

This vegetable is not unlike a turnip in flavor and appearance although it is not in fact a root, but a swelling of the stem near the base.

To prepare: Kohlrabi can be cooked in any of the ways used for turnips, but has a rather more delicate flavor. It is best sliced and cooked for a few minutes in fat, then covered with stock and simmered until tender, about 30 minutes. The leaves can be cooked separately, chopped and used as garnish. It can also be made into purée or fritters, or grated and eaten raw in salads.

LEEKS

The leek is one of the most versatile and useful vegetables in the kitchen; it is valuable both as a flavoring agent for other food, and as a vegetable food in its own right. It is good combined with carrots, or with tomatoes, it goes exceptionally well with lamb, and is delicious in cheese dishes cooked with cream. It makes exquisite soups, such as *vichyssoise* and the French *soupe a la bonne femme.* It is excellent in pastry dishes.

When young, leeks are good eaten cold dressed with a *sauce vinaigrette*.

To prepare: After washing the leeks, cut them in slices an inch thick. Bring an inch of lightly salted water to a boil in a broad heavy pan and throw in the leeks. Cover the pan and cook briskly for 10 minutes, shaking the pan from side to side occasionally. Check to make sure that the water is not boiling away. When the time is up, they should be perfectly tender, with only a minimum of water left to throw away. Toss them over low heat to dry them out, then add a lump of butter, some salt and plenty of black pepper.

LENTILS

The lentil is the seed of a small bushy plant, which grows not more than 1½ feet high. It is a native of the Mediterranean shores, and has been cultivated since Roman times. It is very nutritious, being full of iron and vitamin B. The seeds are borne in tiny pods, and should be stored in the pods until they are to be marketed. Lentils vary in color from an orangey-yellow to green and brown. The orange ones are least satisfactory from the point of view of cooking. They have very little flavor, and quickly disintegrate into a mush. Both the green and brown ones, which can be found in foreign shops, are a great improvement.

To prepare: Lentils do not need soaking, but careful washing and picking over in a colander to remove any little stones and discolored seeds. They should be covered with cold water with an inch or two to spare and brought very slowly to a boil. Simmer for 50 minutes to 1 hour, until they are soft, adding salt towards the end of the cooking. Drain them, reserving the liquid for soup, and add some butter and seasoning of salt and black pepper, and possibly some soy sauce to taste. They can also be cooked in butter with a chopped onion and clove of garlic before they are simmered. If they are to be eaten alone, the latter method is better, but for adding to other dishes, the first is more suitable.

Lentils make marvelous soups, either alone or mixed with other vegetables. They are also good served alone, garnished with hard-boiled eggs or croutons, and strips of bacon. Lentils are very good cold, dressed with oil and vinegar while still hot, and eaten before they have completely cooled. They are good wth sausages of all kinds; they have a comforting, warming quality that is especially welcome in cold weather. There is also a well-known Indian dish called *dhal*, which is composed of orange lentils cooked almost to a mush and served with curry.

LETTUCE

Lettuce comes from the East, probably from India or other parts of Asia. Its origins are so ancient that they are obscure, but it was cultivated in Greek and Roman times. The innumerable varieties fall into three main categories: the round, or cabbage, lettuce; romaine lettuce; and cutting lettuce, rarely found in the United States. The first two are universally known; the latter is a useful salad vegetable as it does not form a head.

To prepare: Lettuce must be carefully cleaned before cooking. If it is used raw in salads, it should be dried.

LIMA BEANS

As their name suggests, these are a native of South America. Originally a tall climbing plant like the English runner bean, they have now been developed in dwarf bush varieties, taking less space in the garden.

To prepare: Bring a little lightly salted water to a boil in a saucepan, throw in the beans and cover the pan. Simmer until tender—about 30 minutes—then drain off the water and add a lump of butter, or some cream or sour cream.

Season well with salt and black pepper and serve immediately.

To make the Indian dish succotash, mix the cooked beans with an equal amount of freshly cooked corn. Add butter, salt and black pepper and serve. Do not attempt to substitute canned lima beans for fresh ones, as they are too starchy to mix with the already starchy corn.

The field mushroom is an edible fungus which grows wild in meadows in the late summer and early autumn, particularly after a spell of damp weather. They are also grown commercially in the United States, and can be bought year-round. They are sold at two stages; first, as button mushrooms, and later, when they have developed a larger flat cap. When freshly picked the gills on the underside of the cap are a delicate shade of buff pink; by the time they reach the shops this has turned to brown. The flavor of the forced variety is not so fine as that of the wild one, which also benefits from being cooked shortly after picking. They should never be kept for any length of time as they quickly deteriorate.

To prepare: When young and very fresh, mushrooms can be eaten raw; sliced and dressed with oil and lemon juice, they make a delicious salad. They can also be cooked, in a variety of different ways: fried, grilled, baked, or stewed in their own juice. They are invaluable as a flavor to enhance other foods. They make an excellent sauce, and are a favorite ingredient of many classic French dishes.

Dried mushrooms are a useful stand-by. The flavor is often better than commercially-grown, fresh mushrooms, but they are only suitable for certain dishes. They need half an hour's soaking before cooking, and are excellent for adding to stews and casseroles or a sauce

MUSHROOM

for spaghetti. Dried mushrooms are a different variety from fresh mushrooms.

MUSTARD GREENS

Popular in the South where they are one of the main ingredients of soul-food cookery, mustard greens are similar to collards, but more tender and with a more delicate tangy flavor.
To prepare: See KALE.

OKRA

A native of the West Indies, okra is also grown extensively in South America where it is known as "gombo." In England it is sometimes called "lady's fingers." The word "gumbo" is also used in the South to denote a soup or stew containing okra. Okra also figures in Middle Eastern cooking. Okra is an annual plant growing to a height of 2 or 3 feet, with long narrow spherical pods. These are somewhat like chili peppers in appearance, but much longer.
To prepare: The pods are sliced or cooked whole; they are usually cooked in oil, and are often mixed with onions, tomatoes, eggplant, and peppers.

ONION

The onion originally came from Central Asia, and has been for many centuries the most important vegetable from the culinary point of view. It is hard to think of any country where it does not figure largely in the cuisine, while it would be almost impossible to create any dish of the classic French cooking without making use of the onion in one of its forms. (The family also includes the shallot, leek and garlic.) It has become so accepted as a vital flavoring agent for so many dishes, including fish, poultry, game and meat, that there is hardly a savory sauce that does not include some form of onion. Soups, stews, casseroles and court-bouillons all rely heavily on the onion, which is also used in vegetable dishes. It is useful in almost all its stages of growth: first, as seedlings, as a substitute for scallions; later, the medium-sized bulb; and finally the giant Spanish onion. The flavor becomes milder as the size increases, which is why many people prefer the Spanish onion for most purposes, especially if it is to be eaten raw.

To prepare: Onions can be steamed, boiled, baked, sauteed in shallow fat or deep-fried in batter, stewed or broiled. Left whole they take a long time to become tender, so they are usually sliced or chopped. Raw onions can be thinly sliced, minced or grated, and eaten in salads of raw or cooked vegetables. The juice can be extracted by squeezing, and used as a flavoring agent. They combine extremely well with potatoes and tomatoes, and they go particularly well with lamb, mutton and beef.

PARSNIPS

Parsnips are a long knobby white root. They make a good substitute for potatoes, and are an excellent choice if only one vegetable dish is to be served. They have a great affinity with butter.

To prepare: Parsnips should be pared thinly and cut in chunks; peel them only shortly before cooking and leave covered in cold water. To cook, cover with cold water, add a little salt and bring to a boil. Simmer until tender when pierced with a skewer—20–30 minutes, depending on the size of the pieces. Drain them well and dry them out over low heat. Add a generous lump of butter and a handful of chopped parsley, and season carefully with salt and black pepper. When all are well coated, serve immediately. A little brown sugar can be added instead of the parsley to bring out their sweetness. They can also be roasted in the oven, like potatoes, or boiled and drained, then made into a purée, either alone or mixed with potatoes. Reheated and beaten with butter, a little cream and plenty of salt and black pepper, they make a delicious accompaniment to grilled steaks. No other vegetable is needed.

PEAS

The pea is an annual that has been widely grown throughout the world, except for the tropics, since antiquity. It is a popular vegetable, and makes a good accompaniment to most meats, fish, and poultry.

Peas are at their best in June and July, although the season continues into early autumn during mild weather. Unfortunately manufacturers of frozen peas get the pick of the market, and really excellent fresh peas are not often available in the shops.

Varieties that are grown especially for the sake of their pods recently became popular in the United States and Europe under the name of "sugar peas," or "snow peas," although they have long been used in Chinese cookery.

To prepare: As peas are only at their best for a short time, it is best to cook them as simply as possible, usually dispensing with any additional flavor, even the classic sprig of mint. When very young, peas need only 4—6 minutes cooking in already boiling very lightly salted water. Drain them quickly and serve in a hot dish with a lump of butter and a pinch of sugar.

During the late summer they lose their initial freshness and delicacy of flavor, and can then be treated differently, made into soups and purées, timbales and mousses, or cooked à la française, with tiny onions and lettuce leaves.

PEPPER

Also known as the sweet pepper, bell pepper, or pimiento, this must not be confused with the Spanish pepper. It is a native of South America, and is a tender plant unable to withstand the cold. It is also widely grown in Mediterranean countries, particularly Spain, southern France, Italy and northern Africa. Recent developments have produced a more hardy variety which can be grown with care in the United States, but it almost always needs some artificial heat to start growing. Green and red peppers are in fact the same plant; the flesh starts green and turns scarlet gradually as it ripens. They are popular in Central European countries, like Hungary. They are mainly used in Provençal-type dishes, stewed in oil with garlic, mixed with onions, tomatoes, eggplant or zucchini. They are also found in stews like the Hungarian *goulash*, or in dishes of stuffed vegetables, either hot or cold. They are also much used in salads, as they can be eaten both raw and cooked.

To prepare: The seeds must always be discarded, along with the stalk and the fibrous interior. The seeds in particular have a bitter taste. Many people find peppers hard to digest raw, in which case they can be peeled by placing under a hot grill (broiler) until the skin has blackened, when it peels away easily. This totally alters their character; they lose their slightly bitter taste and crisp quality and become sweet and of a meltingly soft consistency.

POTATO

The potato was originally a native of South America, although it is now widely grown throughout the world. There are several hundred different types of potato, yet in a store, it is rare to find more than two varieties to choose from. Potatoes fall into two main types: the firm-fleshed waxy variety and the mealy floury-fleshed one. The former are ideal for dishes where the potato must keep its consistency, as in gratins and other dishes of sliced potatoes, while the latter are essential for purées. New potatoes are always waxy, and cannot be made into purées as they form a glutinous sticky paste. Most of the vitamin content of the potato—vitamin C and various minerals—lies just beneath the surface of the skin. For this reason, they should be cooked in their skins whenever possible; if they must be peeled, this can be done after cooking without so much wastage.

To prepare: Scrub the potatoes well, removing any eyes. Put them in a large pan with plenty of cold salted water. Bring to a boil uncovered, and boil gently until almost tender, about 20–25 minutes according to size. When they are still slightly firm when pierced with a skewer, and before they have started to fall to pieces, pour off all the water and cover the pan with a soft clean cloth. Replace over very low heat, and leave for another 5–10 minutes, by which time they will be soft, but not yet disintegrated, with the skin split in a few places to show the delicious floury interior. Serve quite plain, with a dish of butter on the table.

To steam potatoes peel them and cut in half, or quarters if large. Bring some water to a boil in the bottom half of a steamer, and place the potatoes over it when the boiling point is reached. Sprinkle with salt, cover the pan, and cook till soft when pierced with a skewer. They will take slightly longer than when boiled. Do not add butter; the potatoes should be served quite plainly, and are particularly delicious with any dish in a rich sauce or with fish.

To bake potatoes, scrub them well and dry in a cloth. Rub the skins lightly with oil or softened butter. Put the potatoes in an oven preheated to 400 degrees, laying them on the rack. Cook for 1 hour, by which time all but the most gigantic will be soft. Test by squeezing them gently with a cloth, or piercing with a fork. They should not be kept waiting too long or the skins will toughen. Cut a cross in the top to allow the steam to escape and serve as soon as possible, with plenty of butter or a bowl of sour cream mixed with chopped chives.

In addition to the innumerable ways of cooking potatoes, they can be used as the base for a large range of dishes by mixing a dry potato purée with eggs and flour to form a dough; this can be made into scones, pancakes fritters, gnocchi, soufflés, pastry and bread. The potato adapts itself well to so many flavors, without being overly assertive.

PUMPKIN

The pumpkin is one of a huge family of plants, some of which are classified as vegetables, others as fruits. They include cucumber, squash, zucchini, melon and a whole range of ornamental gourds. Fresh pumpkin itself is not much used for cooking nowadays, but rather it is grown for decorative purposes. It is enormously popular as part of the classic American dessert, pumpkin pie. Pumpkin can also be made into a good soup.
To prepare: See SQUASH.

RADISH

The radish is a native of Southern Asia. The most common sort is the red radish, but there is also a black radish, which should be peeled before eating, then treated exactly like the red one. White-fleshed and yellow varieties have recently been developed. Radishes come in shapes varying from round to long and narrow. The radish is full of minerals and vitamins A and C. Their crunchy texture is generally popular; they also make a good cocktail snack.
To prepare: Radishes are almost always eaten raw; they can, in fact, be cooked in boiling water for 5—6 minutes, but they lose the crisp texture that is their most appealing feature. In France, they are served as an hors-d'oeuvre, alone, with coarse salt and fresh unsalted butter.

They should be well scrubbed, the root end trimmed, and a neat bunch of leaves left with which to hold them. They are also good sliced and scattered over a mixed salad, or grated and mixed with a *sauce remoulade*.

RED CABBAGE

A useful winter vegetable, red cabbage is rich in vitamin C, especially when eaten raw. It forms a central part of the cuisine of Poland, Hungary, Austria and neighboring Central European countries, where it is often served as an accompaniment to game. It is also very good served with pork or bacon, and with sausages.

To prepare: Red cabbage can be shredded and eaten raw in salads. Some people parboil it to make it more digestible. Vinegar or lemon juice must be added to the water to preserve the color when it is cooked this way. It should first be cut in quarters, and the outer leaves and central core removed. After washing and draining, the quarters can be thinly sliced. It is now ready to be eaten raw or cooked. Red cabbage responds to long slow cooking in the oven or on top of the stove, moistened with fat and some good stock. It is excellent with the addition of other flavors: chopped apples, crushed juniper berries, garlic and caraway seeds are good, as are a little wine vinegar, sugar, or some yoghurt or sour cream added at the end of the cooking. (Yoghurt must be first mixed with a little flour to prevent it from separating.) Like *sauerkraut*, red cabbage improves by being made in advance and reheated.

ROMAINE

See LETTUCE.

RUTABAGA

Rutabaga is a member of the huge cabbage family and is similar to the kohlrabi, in that the edible part is an underground swelling of the stem rather than an actual root. Its flesh is yellow, as opposed to the white flesh of the turnip.

To prepare: Rutabaga is prepared and cooked exactly like a turnip. The tops also make an excellent green vegetable if picked while still young and tender. They should be cooked till just tender in boiling salted water, well drained, chopped and tossed in melted butter with salt and black pepper. Ordinary turnip tops can be cooked in the same way, but rutabaga tops have a better flavor.

SALSIFY

Also known as the oyster plant or vegetable oyster, salsify is a biennial plant, a native of Europe, that produces a long tapering root whose white flesh has a subtle and unusual flavor.

To prepare: Pare the roots and cut in chunks. Leave covered with cold water with a drop of vinegar or lemon juice until ready to cook or it will discolor. To cook cover the pieces of salsify with lightly salted cold water, bring to a boil and cook until tender, about 30—45 minutes. Drain, then toss in butter and sprinkle with finely chopped chervil or parsley before serving. The blackskinned variety of salsify called scorzonera actually has a better flavor, but is more troublesome to cook. See SCORZONERA.

SAVOY

A variety of cabbage. *See* GREEN CABBAGE.

SCALLION

The scallion is a special variety of onion that matures while still very small. Scallions are almost always used raw, either whole with other crudites or sliced in salads. They can be cooked, but usually are used only as an addition and flavoring to another dish, such as the Irish potato dish called "champ."

SCORZONERA

This is the black-skinned variety of salsify; it differs slightly in that the roots are thicker and covered with a hard black skin, but the flesh is still white. It is generally thought to have the better flavor, but it is troublesome to cook, as it must be peeled after cooking and the soft white flesh tends to fall to pieces, often scalding fingers, while one tries to remove every particle of black skin. It is well worth the trouble to prepare in small quantities, perhaps to serve 3—4. *To prepare:* Scrub the roots well with a stiff brush and trim the ends with a sharp knife. If you have a long enough pan to accommodate them, do not cut the roots, but cook them whole. Measure enough water to cover the roots, salt it lightly, and bring it to a boil. Drop in the scorzonera, bring back to a boil, and boil till tender—about 35—40 minutes. Lift it out and drain. When it is cool enough to handle, scrape off the skin with a small knife and cut the roots in pieces about 1½ inches long. To serve, reheat by tossing in a little butter, and add a few drops of lemon juice or a couple of spoonfuls of chopped fresh herbs— chervil is ideal. Or leave the scorzonera whole, lay in a shallow dish and cover with a *sauce Mornay* (see pp. 139—140), or a cheese soufflé sauce (see p. 133). The roots also can be cut in pieces dipped in any of the batters listed on pages 49—50, and fried in deep fat. Serve with quarters of lemon.

SEA KALE

A native of Western Europe, sea kale originally grew along the seashores and is now cultivated. The part of the plant that is eaten is the stem, broad, white and curved, culminating in a tiny clump of leaves. This is a vegetable delicacy. *To prepare:* Lower gently into boiling lightly salted water, and simmer until tender. Carefully drain and serve while hot. A bowl of melted butter should be passed with this food.

SEAWEED

See CARRAGEEN.

SHALLOT

The shallot is a native of Palestine, and is actually closer to garlic in its method of growth than the onion. The bulb divides itself into a number of cloves, as does garlic, and does not produce seed, as does the onion. It is used primarily as flavoring, and is considered more suitable than the onion for delicate sauces. It is much used in French cuisine.

To prepare: Shallots should always be finely minced or chopped, and they must be cooked gently without allowing them to brown, as browning gives a bitter taste to the finished dish.

SNOW PEAS

Also known as sugar peas, these are an edible podded variety of pea that has long been used in Chinese cookery.

To prepare: The peas simply need the ends pinched off; if they are gathered while still young, there should be no stringy parts at all. Cook them in a broad heavy pan, either whole or cut across in squares, with just enough water to cover the bottom of the pan. Put a lump of butter on the top, and a sprinkling of salt and sugar. Bring to a boil and cook for 4—6 minutes, until they are tender but still crisp. Put them in a serving dish, boil the juice to reduce it to a couple of spoonfuls, and pour it over them.

SORREL

There are several different varieties of sorrel; the one that grows wild is rather bitter. The sort that is generally cultivated is the French broad-leafed sorrel.

To prepare: Sorrel makes a most useful and unusual addition to many summer dishes, either alone, or mixed with other greens such as spinach, dandelion, watercress or lettuce. Tender, young sorrel leaves are delicious sliced and eaten raw mixed with crumbled bacon in a salad. If sorrel is cooked, allow ½ pound per person, as it shrinks as much as spinach. Sorrel also is cooked like spinach. It then makes an excellent purée, and with cream and butter added, is good served with *oeufs mollets* or under poached eggs for a light luncheon dish. It can be mixed with spinach when making a spinach soufflé or made into a delicate soup. Its slightly bitter taste goes well with the blandness of eggs, and it can be used to advantage as the filling for an omelette or as garnish for a dish of scrambled eggs.

SOYBEANS

This plant is a native of China, where it is still grown extensively. It is the most nutritious and easily digested of all the beans, and has become one of the favorite foods of people interested in health foods. It contains large amounts of vitamins B and E, plus a very high degree of minerals, especially calcium and iron. It is richer in protein and fat than almost any other food, including meat, yet is low in starch, and it is ideal for certain diets. It is the basis of soy sauce, and is also made into a flour and an oil.

To prepare: Follow directions for haricot beans.

SPINACH

A native of Persia, spinach has been grown in France since the fourteenth century, and in England since the sixteenth. It has always been popular, and is a very valuable source of iron, as well as vitamins B and C. There are two sorts, winter and summer spinach, and between them it is in season almost all year-round, except for autumn. Summer spinach is far the more delicate of the two, with soft green leaves and stalks, and a lighter flavor, while the winter variety is coarser both in texture and in flavor. It is usually better to discard the stalks of the winter spinach before cooking.

To prepare: In the United States, France, and Italy, spinach is often eaten raw as a salad. In cooking it must be remembered that spinach shrinks amazingly, and at least ½ pound per person should be allowed. It must be very well washed, in three or four different waters. There are two schools of thought about the best way to cook spinach. One way is to rub a heavy pan with a piece of butter and pile in the spinach leaves with only the drops of water left on the leaves after washing. They must be cooked over low heat for 4–7 minutes. Stir once or twice with a wooden spoon.

Another method is to throw the leaves into a large pan of boiling water and cook till just tender. In either case the spinach must be very well drained in a colander, pressing out the water with the back of a spoon. If left to cool slightly, it can be squeezed between the hands. After draining it can be served as is with lemon juice or used in a more elaborate recipe.

SPLIT PEAS

These are dried peas, which are useful during the winter months as a source of vitamin B. They have been used in England for hundreds of years to make "pease pudding," a traditional accompaniment to boiled bacon. Dried peas have a special affinity for ham and bacon; an excellent winter soup can be made with split peas, using the bone and scraps of a ham for flavor.

To prepare: Split peas are cooked in the same way as lentils; they do not require soaking, but should be well picked over and washed in a colander under running water. Put them in a pan, cover with plenty of cold water, add a sliced onion, carrot, leek, celery stalk, or whatever is available in the way of flavoring vegetables, and bring very slowly to a boil. Simmer gently until they are soft when crushed, but not reduced to a mush; add salt towards the end of the cooking. They will probably take about 45 minutes to become tender. Drain them well, unless making a soup, and reheat stirring in a lump of butter or a little cream, and plenty of salt and black pepper. They can be made into a good purée by pushing through a vegetable mill, then reheating. The purée is excellent with sausages.

SPRUE

This is the technical name for the thinnings from asparagus beds, which can often be bought cheaply either directly from asparagus farms or from a produce market. The thin green stalks can be made into many delicious dishes at a very reasonable cost.

To prepare: Cooked like asparagus, but more briefly, they are delicious served as a bed for poached eggs, covered with *sauce hollandaise*. They can also be used for asparagus soups, or any of the dishes requiring asparagus tips as a garnish.

SQUASH

Squash is a popular vegetable, available in varying forms year-round. Summer squashes come in all shapes and colors, and have a delicate thin skin which can be pierced with the finger nail. They include straight neck squash, crooked neck squash, cymling, and zucchini.

Winter squash come into season in the autumn and are available until early spring. With the exception of the butternut squash, they have hard skins. They include golden delicious, acorn, buttercup or turban, and Hubbard squash. They store well, especially the Hubbard squash.

To prepare: Summer squash should be cooked while still young, before the seeds have had time to form. They do not store well, but should be cooked soon after purchase. Peel or not, as you wish, then steam, poach, sauté or stew gently in their own juice till tender. Season well before serving.

Before cooking winter squash, the seeds should be removed, after which the squash can be peeled and cut in pieces, or it can be baked in the oven for 30—45 minutes and the flesh removed from the shell after cooking. Squash lend themselves well to stuffing with mixtures of rice, meat or vegetables.

SWEET CORN

Sweet corn was a staple food of some American Indian groups and was adopted by the first European settlers to avoid starvation. It became one of the favorite American dishes, and its popularity has only recently spread to England. Corn has a very high content of both sugar and starch.

To prepare: The end of the stalk should be trimmed and the husk removed. If cooked immediately after picking, corn-on-the-cob needs only 5—8 minutes in boiling water to become tender; the following day it will need 20—30 minutes. Corn can also be grilled or baked in the oven.

To remove corn from the cob, hold the cobs downwards onto the table and slice the kernels off the cob with a sharp knife, as close to the cob as possible. This is easily done, and is far preferable to using frozen or canned corn, which loses much of its sweet milky taste. When cooked off the cob, corn needs only a short cooking in a little lightly salted water, brought to a boil before adding the corn.

SWEET POTATO

The sweet potato originated in South America. There are two types: the ordinary, or Jersey, sweet potato and the yam. The former has a pale yellow flesh of a dry floury consistency, while the flesh of the yam is orange in color and more oily. Both are treated in identical ways. The sweet potato is rich in vitamin C, and takes the place of the ordinary potato in the diet of most tropical countries.

To prepare: The potatoes should be well washed or scrubbed before cooking; in most cases they are peeled after cooking. They can be cooked very much like the ordinary potato: boiled, baked, fried, or made into a purée. To boil: cut in pieces if large, or leave whole. Cover with cold salted water and boil till soft. Drain well, add butter, salt and black pepper, or make into a puree. To bake: heat the oven to 400 degrees, lay the scrubbed potatoes on the oven rack, and bake for 45−60 minutes, until soft when squeezed with a cloth or pierced with a fork. Serve with butter, salt and black pepper. To fry: peel the potatoes and cut them in slices. Shallow fry in butter till soft, turning often. Season with salt and black pepper.

SWISS CHARD

Also known as sea kale beet, white beet or spinach beet, this is a variety of beet grown for the sake of the central rib of the leaf, which is called the chard. Easy to grow, and rich in vitamin C, this useful vegetable is especially popular in France.

To prepare: Both the leaf and the stem are nutritious and have a delicate flavor, but they are best cooked separately. The leaf should be cut away from the chard and cooked in an absolute minimum of water. Put a couple of tablespoons of water in a heavy pan and pack in the leaves. Bring the water to a boil and cook gently, turning the leaves over as the bottom ones release their moisture, until all are wilted and tender. Drain well, pressing out excess liquid, and serve with a little melted butter seasoned with salt and black pepper. The ribs should be left whole and cooked like sea kale. Bring enough lightly salted water just to cover them to a boil in a broad pan or in a steamer, and cook them gently until tender. Drain them well, and serve them on a dish with melted butter poured over them. If very large, they can be cut into pieces after cooking. Some varieties (spinach beet, for instance) do not produce such large ribs and can be cooked together. Cut the leaves across, including the chard, in ½-inch pieces, and cook in already boiling lightly salted water until just tender; drain and reheat in seasoned melted butter.

A native of South America, the tomato is, strictly speaking, a fruit, but it is always treated as a vegetable. Originally known as a "love apple"—it was thought to have aphrodisiacal qualities—the tomato was introduced to England in the sixteenth century. It had the immediate appeal of a novelty, but its popularity later waned. It was not much used in the United States until the early nineteenth century, by which time it was again popular in England. Its flavor combines well with onions, leeks, garlic, herbs, eggplant, zucchini, and squash while its color lends a pleasing contrast to many pale dishes. A tomato sauce provides the perfect accompaniment to many vegetable dishes such as soufflés and timbales, stuffed green vegetables, and dishes like gnocchi, pancakes, and noodles.

Tomatoes contain valuable minerals and vitamins A and C. They are one of the few vegetables which do not suffer from canning; indeed, a good canned tomato often has more flavor than a mediocre fresh one. Tomatoes need a lot of heat to bring out their true flavor, which perhaps explains why the Italian plumshaped tomato, sold exclusively in cans, is so good. The type generally grown throughout the

TOMATO

United States is the smooth-skinned round tomato, with a lot of juice. At the peak of the tomato season, one may find the beefsteak tomato. Very large, with a rather ugly appearance, deeply ridged skin and a much drier flesh, it has an excellent flavor and is better for all dishes, especially for stuffing. There is also a tiny cherry tomato, used as a garnish and in salads, and the green tomato, which is often fried.

To prepare: Unless they are to be cooked in the oven or broiled, tomatoes should always be skinned before cooking. This is quickly done by pouring boiling water over them and leaving for 1 minute, then plunging them into cold water. The skin will then slip off easily. They can be cooked in a multitude of ways: fried in butter, cut in half and grilled, baked in the oven either whole or sliced, steamed or stewed in their own juice.

TRUFFLE

There are three main sorts of truffles, by far the most highly esteemed being the black truffle which is found in France, particularly in the area round Périgord. The truffle, a form of fungus, has some of the magical qualities of the wild mushroom in that it has defied all attempts to cultivate it. The nearest approach to cultivation has been to make plantations of the trees they prefer to grow under in places where the soil is suitable. Truffles are notoriously difficult to find, and special dogs and pigs are used to "nose" them out.

In the north of Italy there is a white truffle which is found in the autumn. It is quite different from the black, both in texture and flavor. It has a sweet nutty taste, like a cross between a nut and a mushroom, and has a hard consistency. Its uses are limited, as it is only eaten raw and is usually reserved as a garnish for noodles, risotto or scrambled eggs. It should be cut in the thinnest possible slices and scattered over the cooked dish.

Even the best French truffle has very little actual flavor of its own, but it has a curious quality of bringing out the flavors of other foods, particularly poultry and patés. It is almost always used in small quantities as a garnish, as it has great visual appeal. Its glossy black surface lends a very pleasing appearance to a ham mousse, for example. In England and the United States they can only be bought canned, either whole, or in a cheaper version which is the peelings. In Paris they can be bought fresh during the early winters. They are so extremely expensive now that they are rarely cooked as they used to be, as a dish in their own right. (They were poached in champagne, or a mixture of champagne and veal stock, for 10–15 minutes, and served wrapped in a napkin.)

TURNIP

Turnips have been cultivated since the earliest times, and it is hard to know what was their actual country of origin. There are many different varieties, but they fall into two main types: the round or slightly flattened turnip which is mainly grown in England and the United States, and the oval-shaped root, rather like a fat carrot, which is popular in France. However tiny the round ones are, they may still have a hard core which is impossible to make tender by cooking if they have been incorrectly grown.

To prepare: Young turnips make delicious eating raw, as crudités; they have a sweet taste and crisp texture that is ideal for this purpose. To be eaten at their best they should be very thinly pared, cut in slices and chilled. To cook, they should be cut in halves, quarters, or chunks according to their size. Like all root vegetables they should be covered with cold water, lightly salted, brought to a boil and cooked until tender.

It is hard to give exact timing, as so much depends on the age of the turnip. After 10 minutes they should be tested frequently with a fork. If allowed to cook for too long they will disintegrate into a watery mass. They should be well drained, then tossed in melting butter with freshly chopped parsley. They can also be made into a delicious purée, which first must be well dried out, then mixed with butter and cream and carefully seasoned with salt and black pepper. Turnips also make excellent purées mixed with other root vegetables, such as carrots, parsnips or rutabagas, or with potatoes. Turnips have an affinity with fat, and should always have a generous lump of butter added. They are the classic accompaniment to foods with a high fat content, such as duck or mutton.

Turnip tops, the young sprouting leaves, are also edible. They should be thrown into boiling salted water, cooked briskly for 8–10 minutes, drained, chopped, and returned to the pan with a lump of butter, salt and pepper.

WATERCRESS

Watercress is a native plant of the British Isles, where it can be found growing wild in streams. It is now grown commercially in an improved variety with much larger leaves, and is available all the year round. It is too often used merely as a garnish, left uneaten on the plate after the steak has been consumed. This is sad, as it is not only delicious, both as a salad vegetable and a cooked food, but is also extremely rich in iron. It makes excellent sandwiches, a classic soup, and a pretty pale green sauce to serve over *oeufs mollets*. It looks extremely decorative mixed with paler green leaves in a salad, while adding its own slightly astringent flavor.

To prepare: See SPINACH.

This is always shredded or very thinly sliced and eaten raw. It makes the classic American dish, cole slaw, and is also good mixed with other grated raw vegetables, fruit and nuts. It goes a surprisingly long way, and a quarter of a head makes quite a substantial dish as it is very filling. It is rich in vitamin C. White cabbage is also made into the classic German dish, sauerkraut, finely shredded white cabbage which has been pickled in brine. It is the national dish of Alsace, and many of the Central European countries. Many families prepare their own version each year in a barrel, and consume it during the winter months. The pickling process makes it more easily digested than it would otherwise be; it can even be well-drained and rinsed and eaten raw as a salad.

To prepare: The most usual way of cooking sauerkraut is a slow lengthy process in a heavy casserole in the oven, with additions of fat, stock, and juniper berries or caraway seeds. It is usually served with a variety of smoked and fresh meat, mostly pork. Boiled ham or bacon, pigs' feet, fresh or smoked sausages, or pork chops can be served on a huge platter of sauerkraut, surrounded with boiled potatoes. This extremely hearty meal, served with a variety of mustards, is the specialty of many of the Paris brasseries. Sauerkraut also goes well with game, and is often served in Austria as an accompaniment to venison, wild boar, or pheasant. It can be bought straight from the barrel in some foreign delicatessens and in cans.

WHITE CABBAGE

One of the two main types of sweet potato. See SWEET POTATO.

YAM

Zucchini is a cultivated form of squash especially developed to give a succession of small fruits rather than one mammoth show. Although

ZUCCHINI

larger plants are still perfectly edible, the smaller ones are tastier.

To prepare: Zucchini can be cooked in a variety of different ways, fried whole or sliced in butter or oil, poached, stewed in their own juice or baked in the oven. They combine well with tomatoes and herbs such as basil, dill, and chervil. They also go well with other Mediterranean vegetables such as eggplant, sweet peppers, onions, and garlic. They are good flavored with cheese, but it should be a subtle and delicate one such as Parmesan or Gruyère, rather than a strong cheddar. They can be peeled or not, left whole or cut in slices. The male flowers of the plant can also be cooked and make a very pretty dish. They can either be dipped in batter and deep-fried or stuffed and fried or baked.

[13]

Herb Encyclopedia

Herbs are of immense importance in vegetable cookery, and anyone with any space at all, even a broad windowsill capable of accommodating some large pots, would be wise to grow at least a few herbs during the summer months. It is hard to find anything more unusual than fresh parsley or chives in the stores, and they are often ridiculously expensive.

Varieties of herbs that are especially valuable to the vegetable cook include basil, chervil, chives, dill, marjoram, at least one kind of mint, parsley, tarragon, and thyme. These herbs are useful for their light, fresh taste and combine well with vegetable dishes. Others, which have stronger flavors and should be reserved for meat and fish dishes, are rosemary, bay, and sage.

Chervil and dill are annuals, and they must be started over each spring. Tarragon is too fragile to survive winter on most windowsills. But all these herbs are worth trying to grow at least once.

Dried herbs can be substituted, of course, in any recipe, but they must be used in much smaller quantities. A fairly good rule of thumb is to reduce the amount of fresh herbs by one-half when substituting dried herbs.

ANGELICA

The roots of the angelica, a plant native to the Alps, were once thought to have medicinal qualities; they were used in seventeenth-century England to prevent the plague. They were also thought to be a protection against evil spirits.

In its native habitat it grows more than four feet high, with large, deeply indented leaves and yellow flowers. A white-flowered variety called "sylvestris" grows wild in England. It can easily be grown from seed, which should be planted in July or August. It will not flower until the second year, after which it should be dug up and replanted, as it will run to seed.

The stems are crystallized and used as a decoration for cakes; in some parts of Europe the leaves are eaten as a vegetable.

ANISE

A native of Greece and Egypt, it is hard to say whether anise is technically an herb or a spice. It has been used since ancient times both medicinally and as a seasoning; the Romans made a spiced cake using it as one of the spices. It was also used to flavor bread and soups, and was supposed to cure headaches and indigestion. A pretty plant, it grows about a foot high with very fine leaves and flowers like fennel or dill. It grows easily in a warm sheltered spot.

BALM

Also known as lemon balm, this plant has a refreshing scent and flavor. It is a native of southern Europe. It is a pretty bushy plant, with tiny leaves of bright green which release their exquisite lemon scent when crushed. It was formerly used for making wine and as an infusion for herb tea. It was supposed to bring joy and comfort to the spirit, and to cure toothache and asthmatic illnesses. It was also recommended to students to help clear the brain and sharpen the memory. It has not many uses nowadays, but might be included in an herb garden for its delicious scent and appearance.

BASIL

There are many different varieties of basil; the one to choose for culinary purposes is "sweet basil." This variety has a large broad leaf, as opposed to the tiny leaves of the "bush basils." It is a native of India, where the Hindus considered it to be a holy plant and grew it near their temples to protect them from misfortune. In medieval England it was thought to have powers against witchcraft. As a pot-herb it was more highly prized by the French than the English, who used it for its magical qualities.

Coming as it does from a very hot country it is not easily cultivated in more temperate climates, but is very well worth the effort. It needs a lot of sun to develop its true flavor, and benefits from being grown under glass, or even inside a sunny window, at least during the early part of the summer. The leaves should be picked frequently to promote new growth.

It has a special affinity with tomatoes and with all pasta dishes, cheese, and eggs. It is the basic ingredient in the famous Provençal sauce *pistou,* or *pesto* as it is called in Italy. The leaves are pounded in a mortar and then added to grilled tomatoes, pine kernels and Parmesan cheese, according to the version used.

BAY

This is not strictly speaking an herb, but the leaf of the bay tree. Since the French chose to include it in their classic *bouquet garni*, however, it has been treated as such. It has become one of the classic flavorings for many dishes—almost all casseroles of meat, poultry and game, soups and stocks.

BERGAMOT

A variety of mint with lemon-scented leaves, this plant is also known as *mentha citronata*.

BORAGE

Native to Europe and northern Africa, borage is a pretty plant growing about 18 inches high with bright blue flowers in May and June. It was thought by the Romans to be good for the spirits, and was much used as a cure for depression and melancholy. The leaves were also used as a pot-herb, while the flowers were candied. Nowadays its only use is a garnish for Pimms cup and other wine drinks.

CAMOMILE

A tiny low-growing plant with minute white flowers, camomile flourishes by being walked on, and is ideal for small lawns or paths, for instance, throughout an herb garden. It should be rolled with a roller, and only needs occasional clipping. Do not attempt to make a camomile lawn in a shady place, however; the plants will grow tall and straggly, searching for light. In France it is still used to make an herb drink with supposed medicinal qualities, as it has been for many centuries.

CHERVIL

Chervil is a native of southern Europe, and was grown by the Romans, who prized it highly. It is somewhat like parsley, but with a more delicate flavor; also like parsley, it comes in two varieties, the flat-leafed and the curly-leafed. The latter is not often seen nowadays, but is pretty as a garnish. Chervil may be used instead of parsley in many dishes; it is also good in a mixture of herbs, as its flavor is not so strong as to dominate the others, as do basil and tarragon.

A member of the onion family, the chive is a native of southern Europe. Its main use is as a garnish, as it quickly loses its flavor when subjected to heat. The bright green tubular leaves make an attractive decoration for pale dishes, while the sharp onionlike flavor contrasts perfectly with bland creamy foods such as vichyssoise. Chives should always be cut with scissors, rather than chopped with a knife, which spoils their shape and bruises them so that they turn black.

CHIVES

Coriander is usually thought of as a spice, for the seeds are much used in Oriental cookery, but the young leaves can also be used in their fresh state. They are much used in Chinese cookery, where they are also called *hsiang-tsai,* or "Chinese parsley," and in Indian cookery. When crushed they add a hot taste to food that is very popular in the East, where they are added to food as a seasoning after cooking. Ground coriander is available in most stores.

CORIANDER

Dill is an annual plant, native to southern Europe. In appearance much like fennel, it has very fine leaves and flat flower heads containing the seeds. It was formerly used in England as a potherb and in salads, but is now rarely seen, although it is much used in Austria, Hungary, and Poland in a sauce for boiled meat and in conjunction with cucumbers. In Scandinavia it is cooked with boiled potatoes, which are sometimes served with a sprig of dill curled around them. It has a pleasant fresh taste that goes well with eggs and vegetable dishes or as a flavor-

DILL

ing for a cream sauce. It also combines well with mustard, and makes an excellent dish with poached chicken in a mustard and dill sauce. The seeds are used in pickling cucumbers; they can be bought in packets like celery seed and anise seed.

FENNEL

This is the common or garden fennel, as opposed to the wild fennel or *finnochio*, or the Italian fennel that is cultivated for the sake of its swollen root base. The common or garden variety is very similar to dill in appearance, with the same feathery leaves and flat flower heads, but has thicker stalks and a slightly bitter flavor. It is usually used with fish dishes or in a sauce. In medieval times it was the most usual accompaniment to grilled mackerel, either alone or with gooseberries. The seeds were used to flavor liqueurs. It was also used for soup, salads, as a pickling spice, and as an infusion for herb tea.

MARIGOLD

Although no longer thought of as an herb, the marigold always used to be included in herb gardens, and was much used in the kitchen. The petals were added to salads, where they give a pleasing effect, and used as a flavoring for stews and casseroles.

MARJORAM

There are two varieties of marjoram, the "sweet marjoram," which is the most common, and the "French marjoram," or *origanum onites*. Much used in Italian and Greek cooking, where it is known as oregano, it has a delicious flavor that goes particularly well with tomatoes, especially in sauces for spaghetti and pizza, and with fish, eggs, and salads. In Greece a bowl of dried oregano is often served as an accompaniment to a mixed salad with feta cheese. It is also good as a flavoring for ground meat dishes, such as meat loaf and meat balls, and in pâtés. It is easily grown as long as it is planted in a sunny spot. This aromatic plant should be grown from seed planted each spring.

MINT

There are many different varieties of mint, and if there is available space at least two or three varieties should be included in the herb or kitchen garden. The most commonly used is spearmint. This is the old-fashioned English variety, used for the classic dishes such as mint sauce. Apple mint is a particularly decorative variety with its variegated green and white leaves, while eau-de-cologne mint is grown for its delicious pineapple scent when crushed. Ginger mint also has variegated leaves and a warm gingery scent while peppermint has the familiar peppermint smell. A useful variety for the kitchen is *mentha cordifolia,* which has a good flavor for sauces and salads.

In the United States and England mint is only used occasionally, as a sauce for roast lamb and as a flavoring for new potatoes and green peas, but in the Middle East it is the most commonly used herb in the kitchen. Most families dry their own mint, as they prefer to use it in its dried state for most dishes. It is used in far larger quantities there than we are accustomed to, for instance in *tabbouleh,* an Arabic salad entirely composed of parsley and mint. It is also frequently used as a flavoring for salads and sauces, and as a seasoning for grilled meat. It is almost too easy to grow, as the roots have a tendency to spread all over the. garden. It is a good idea to plant it in a flower pot or large tin can, so that the roots are contained; otherwise, it will overrun the whole garden.

PARSLEY

Parsley is one of the most commonly used herbs. Unfortunately it is more often used as a garnish rather than an actual food, although it is full of iron and vitamins. There are three varieties: the flat-leafed or "French parsley," which is supposed to have the best flavor; the curly-leafed or common parsley, most popular as a garnish; and the "Hamburg parsley," grown for the sake of its root, which has an excellent flavor for adding to soups and stews. I am very fond of all three, and like to grow them in large quantities. Parsley makes an attractive hedge for an herb or kitchen garden.

In England it is most often used in parsley sauce, but in the Middle East it is eaten in large quantities in its own right, in salads and vegetable dishes.

In France it has always been included in the classic *bouquet garni*, along with thyme, bay and a piece of celery, for flavoring casseroles, soups, and sauces. In the 1920s and 1930s parsley was often deep-fried and served as a garnish. It is easily grown, but exceedingly slow to germinate, taking seven or eight weeks for the plants to appear.

ROSEMARY

A native of Southern Europe, rosemary grows widely in the south of France, along the shores of the Mediterranean. It is a pretty evergreen plant, with little spikey leaves of greyish-green, and spikes of misty blue flowers. It has a pleasant smell, but its flavor is strong in cooking. It would certainly overpower delicate foods such as most vegetables, but can be delicious used in small quantities when roasting or grilling meat, especially a leg of lamb. A sprig of rosemary is also sometimes used as a brush with which to marinate kebabs, particularly when grilling outdoors.

Sage is another herb that has a flavor and scent too pervasive for frequent use, but it is a pretty plant with silver-grey leaves, and should always be included in the herb garden. Sage is used to season roasts, and is good added to bean dishes.

SAGE

SAVORY

There are two distinct varieties of this plant: the summer savory, which grows from one central stem and has a delicate flavor, and the winter savory, which grows in a bushy shape and is a stronger plant with a more pronounced flavor. Both savories are the classic French accompaniment for dishes of beans, particularly broad beans. Summer savory is an annual, while the more robust winter savory will live through most winters.

Although tarragon came originally from Siberia, the cultivated variety is a delicate plant that has to be nursed through severe winters if it is to survive. It is essential to obtain the right variety of tarragon, that is to say, the true French tarragon, as this is the only one of any use in the kitchen. The other variety, although identical to the eye, has no flavor whatsoever. Tarragon is a favorite among herbs with its unusual and distinctive taste, delicate enough to combine with other herbs, yet equally delicious on its own. It is especially good with chicken; in eggs, especially in omelettes; in cream sauces; with fish, or in salads.

TARRAGON

A native of southern Europe, thyme is connected in most people's minds with the Mediterranean shores, where it flourishes in the dry scrubby vegetation and the great heat of the sun brings out its aromatic scent. There are many different varieties of this charming plant; some have tiny

THYME

white flowers, others pink or mauve, and the leaves can be grey, golden, or variegated. Several of the creeping thymes can be used to excellent effect to make small carpets or paths in gardens. For cooking the best variety is the common thyme, but there is also an interesting variety called *thymus citriodorus*, with an unusual lemon flavor that is excellent with eggs and tomatoes.

Index